Printing Fundamentals

Edited by Alex Glassman

TAPPI PRESS

International Standard Book Number 0-89852-045-2
Library of Congress Catalog Card Number 85-050986

Copyright © 1985 by

TAPPI
Technology Park/Atlanta
P.O. Box 105113, Atlanta, GA 30348, USA

Printed in the United States of America

Preface

This TAPPI PRESS book was originally undertaken in 1960 by the late Dr. Marvin Rogers, then director of research at R.R. Donnelley & Sons, for whom I worked. The book's purpose was to provide better communication between the users of paper, namely printers, and the producers of paper. It was Dr. Rogers' experience and that of other pioneers in the relationship between paper and printers, that when papermakers understand printing and other end-uses of paper, they are better able to direct their energies to producing paper with the right end-use attributes.

Printing Fundamentals is a primer about printing, particularly printing as it relates to paper. For this reason, we have avoided technical details on problems not directly concerned with paper, for example, aesthetic considerations of color and color proofing, copy preparation, and details on preliminary photographic and platemaking operations, perhaps vital to a printer working within the plant and with customers. The book presents information useful as an introduction to a particular subject for a person working in the industry or with a supplier who is a TAPPI member.

The book is divided into sections for easy referencing. Section I discusses principles of contact printing and Section II discusses noncontact printing. These two sections are recommended reading to understand the fundamentals of printing.

Sections III – VIII cover end-use areas: newsprint (III), commercial printing (IV), labels and packaging (V), book publishing (VI), business papers (VII) and board (VIII).

Section IX and Section X are particularly important to all printers and users of paper concerned with printability and performance characteristics of paper. Test methods and terminology describe paper performance and printability in language common to both industries. It is somewhat similar to TAPPI's CA #13 on Production Operation Communication Standards for use by magazine publishers, printers, and papermakers. The book concludes with Section XI which looks at future trends in paper and printing.

Printing Fundmentals was written by authorities with many years of experience in printing or printing-related work. Many of the authors have written texts and textbooks addressed to audiences in their own industries or technical associations. As editor, I have attempted to combine the fundamentals of printing as they exist today, into a useful primer and reference into the future.

My special thanks go to the energetic Printing Committee Chairman in 1979-1980, Dr. Ralph Gordon, and to Dr. Bill Walker, who encouraged me to update, revise, and complete the texts.

Thanks are also due to the companies who employed me from 1960 to 1971, especially R.R. Donnellely in printing, and in paper, Oxford Paper for encouraging me in my TAPPI work. The customers of my consulting firm, including Rolland Paper, International Paper, Rand McNally, Olivetti, and others through 1971-1982, provided me with information helpful in producing Printing Fundamentals.

In actually producing this book, my thanks go to the late Florence B. Glassman (1925-1979), who organized the book into its present format, and to Marc Glassman, who edited many of the sections. Also, thanks are in order for Carolyn Glassman, who secured the final texts, completed the illustrations, and is truly responsible for the realization of the final work. Each spent a great deal of time securing appropriate authors, revising and critically reviewing their texts, and typing and retyping the works.

Printing Fundamentals is dedicated to Dr. Marvin C. Rogers, director of research of R.R. Donnelley & Sons, consultant, president of TAGA, and founder of Photo-Engravers' Research Institute, the leader who started this project in 1960 and carried it on until 1970.

Dr. Rogers and I were supported by our associates at R.R. Donnelley & Sons, and by our leaders, especially the late Elliott Donnelley and Charles W. Lake, Jr., to whom Dr. Rogers and I reported. They inspired us to work closely with the paper industry.

Alex Glassman
Editor

Contents

Section II
Principles of Noncontact Printing   /   49

2   Principles of Noncontact Printing   /   51

Section III
Groundwood Paper Grades   /   73

3   Groundwood Paper Grades   /   75

Section IV
Coated Grades and Commercial Printing / 115

Section VII
Business and Writing Papers / 181

List of Figures

List of Tables

Section I
Principles of Contact (Impression) Printing Processes

Michael H. Bruno, Editor

1
Principles of Contact (Impression) Printing Processes

Michael H. Bruno

Introduction

Contact or *impression* printing describes the processes that use an inked printing plate or image carrier to produce numerous reproductions of an original on paper or other substrates using a device known as a printing press, on which pressure is used to transfer the inked image to the paper. This definition differentiates contact printing from photography, where each print must be processed, and from noncontact printing processes such as electrophotography, thermal imaging, jet printing, and other processes described in Chapter 2.

The invention of modern printing is credited to Johannes Gutenberg who introduced the system of using movable type for printing on a press with ink on paper to the Western world around 1440. Previously, all books and other types of text reproduction were laboriously handwritten by scribes.

The printing industry, including printing, publishing, and packaging, is one of the largest industries in the United States, representing about 3% of the Gross National Product. As the fifth or sixth largest component of the Gross National Product (GNP), the printing industry produces millions of paperback books a day; millions of case-bound books a week; billions of magazines, newspapers, greeting cards, and business forms; millions of catalogs, directories, and maps; and millions of tons of packaging and other printing products each year. In 1982, the printing and publishing industries produced products valued at $39.2 billion in 1972 constant dollars and are expected to increase to $44.3 billion by 1986, representing an annual increase of 3.1% (in real dollars). Packaging is growing at approximately the same rate.

Printing methods

In all printing processes, the image carrier or printing plate consists of two areas: printing or image areas which are inked to produce the image and non-printing or nonimage areas which remain clean or unprinted. There are four methods of printing (Fig. 1.1): *relief*, characterized by letterpress and flexography, where the image area is raised and the nonimage is below the raised surface; *intaglio*, characterized by gravure, where the image consists of tiny wells in a plate or cylinder which holds the ink and the nonimage areas are scraped clean with a metal doctor blade that contacts the smooth outer surface of the plate or cylinder; *planographic*, characterized by lithography, where the printing and nonprinting areas are essentially on the same plane but differ in their receptivity to ink and water: the printing areas accept the ink and the nonprinting areas accept the water; *stencil* or *porous*, characterized by screen printing, where a metal, silk, or nylon screen or a fibrous material is used, on which the nonprinting areas are blocked so the ink only goes through the porous areas which represent the image.

The printing process where ink is transferred directly to the paper is known as *direct printing*. The ink may also be transferred from the inked plate to an intermediate cylinder covered with a rubber blanket which transfers it to the paper or other substrate; this is known as *offset printing*. Letterpress, gravure, and screen printing are almost always direct printing. Lithography, on the other hand, is almost exclusively offset printing and is usually referred to as offset (Fig. 1.2).

A printing press may be flat-bed or rotary (Fig. 1.3). In the flat-bed press, the image carrier, type, or plate, is on a flat bed, which may be either horizontal or vertical. Flat-bed presses are used chiefly for letterpress, screen printing, and for proofing. In a rotary press, the plate is mounted on a cylinder. Plates may also be mounted on a belt, as on a belt press.

Presses are classified as sheet-fed or web-fed (Figs. 1.4, 1.5, 1.6). On a sheet-fed press, sheets of paper are fed into the press one at a time, the impression is made, and the sheet is removed or delivered into a pile. On a web-fed press, the paper is fed from a roll and printing is continuous as the paper passes under the inked plate or blanket on the rotating cylinder. All of the major printing processes can be printed on sheet-fed and web-fed presses.

The printing system

A typical printing job progresses through several steps. These steps are outlined to orient the reader to recognize the various parts of the printing process when they are discussed separately. The procedure described here is for offset lithography; steps for letterpress or gravure will vary.

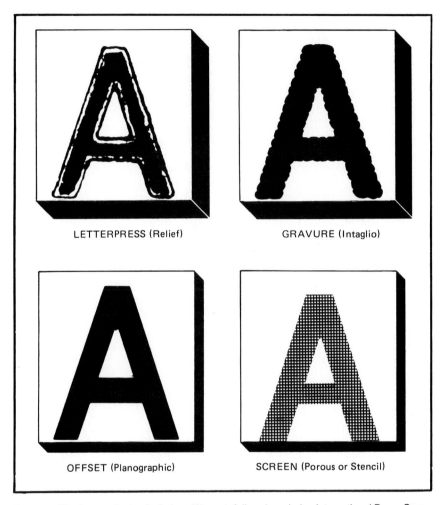

LETTERPRESS (Relief)

GRAVURE (Intaglio)

OFFSET (Planographic)

SCREEN (Porous or Stencil)

Fig. 1.1 The four methods of printing. (We gratefully acknowledge International Paper Company's permission to use the illustrations appearing in its copyrighted publication, *POCKET PAL*® .)

1. The customer, the art department of the printer, or an advertising agency prepares a rough layout or "dummy" of what the final job should look like.

2. The customer, artist, or agency supplies the copy for reproduction. This may contain text copy as typewritten manuscript, line drawings, and photographs marked for final size and cropping, and color prints or transparencies if the job is to be in color. The layout will indicate areas for block or line color if necessary.

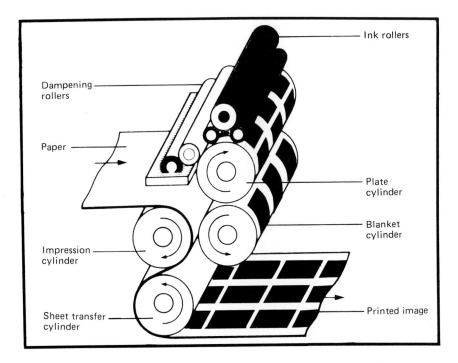

Fig. 1.2 Offset lithography. (We gratefully acknowledge International Paper Company's permission to use the illustrations appearing in its copyrighted publication, *POCKET PAL®* .)

3. The printer or customer prepares a mechanical layout which shows the position and size of all the copy elements for the job on each page, or part of the job.

4. The printer or customer has the copy typeset, preferably on a photo-typesetting machine.

5. The line drawings and photographs are sent to the photographic department where they are photographed to the correct size and shape indicated by crop marks. Prints can be made to size of the line drawings, and these are pasted in position on the mechanical layout. The continuous-tone photographs are converted to halftones, which are kept to be assembled or stripped later on the flat used for the plate-making. Black or red boxes are pasted on the mechanical, indicating the size and position of the halftone illustrations. On some types of work, photographic prints are made from the halftone negatives, or halftone prints are made directly and the prints are pasted up in position on the layout to be photographed with the rest of the copy. The color illustrations would be reproduced as described in the section on color reproduction of this chapter.

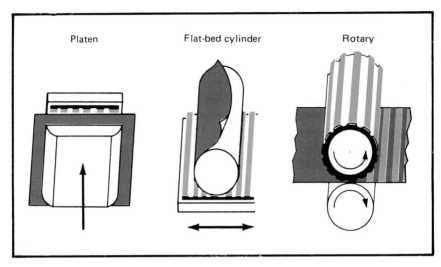

Fig. 1.3   Three types of letterpress. (We gratefully acknowledge International Paper Company's permission to use the illustrations appearing in its copyrighted publication, *POCKET PAL®* .)

6. After all the elements are pasted up on the mechanical, it is photographed at the same size so a complete negative is produced with clear areas representing the places where the halftones, if any, are to be inserted. Depending on the job, the mechanical can represent the whole job, part of the job, or individual pages in book and magazine printing. The assembly of all negatives in position onto a sheet of yellow or orange paper or plastic is known as *stripping* or image assembly in offset lithography, and is called a *flat*. If the job is in color, a separate flat must be prepared for each color. Pin register is used to ensure a satisfactory fit, or register, between flats.

7. The flats are used for exposing the printing plates which are usually the full size of the printing cylinder. Small units or individual negatives can be used to make multiple exposures on the plate using a step-and-repeat procedure or machine. Since negatives have been used in the illustration, the plates must be negative working plates.

8. After the plate is processed, it is mounted on the press and as many copies are printed as needed to complete the order. Usually about 5% paper waste is allowed for each color on a sheet-fed press, unless it is a long run, and then waste is reduced proportionately. Waste is higher on a web press. The waste is needed to allow the pressman to get the job into proper position on the sheet and to get the right color. This is known as *makeready*.

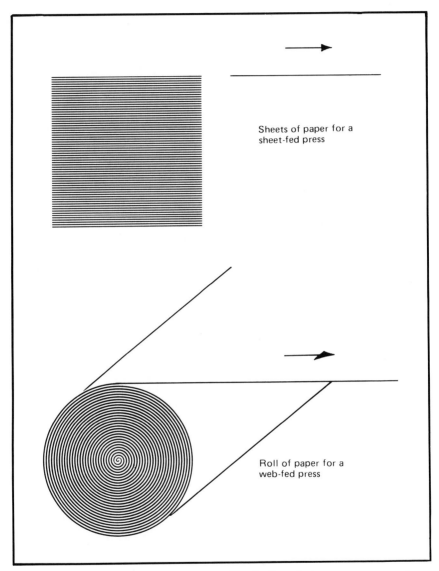

Sheets of paper for a
sheet-fed press

Roll of paper for a
web-fed press

Fig. 1.4 Sheet-fed press and web-fed press "feeding" methods.

9. When the ink is dry on the sheets, further processing such as folding, trimming, cutting, drilling, collating, and/or stitching may be needed, depending on whether the final product is a letterhead, poster, greeting card, folder, magazine, or book.

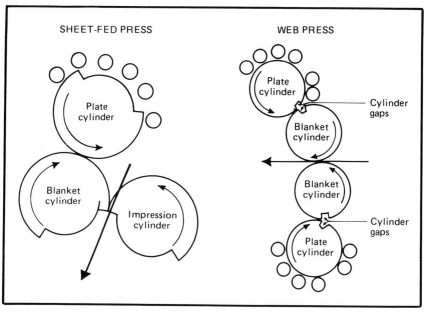

Fig. 1.5 Sheet-fed press and web-fed press printing units.

Preparatory operations

The printing process is divided into two parts: (1) the preparatory or prepress operations, which consist of copy preparation, typesetting, photography, assembly of the films into a layout or form, and platemaking; and (2) printing and finishing, in which the sheets are printed and drilled, collated, folded, etc., into their final form.

Typesetting

Most typesetting or composing in the past was achieved by handsetting individual metal type characters and by machines such as the Linotype invented by Ottmar Mergenthaler in 1886. Machine composition is known as linecasting: the machines cast one line at a time. It is also known as *hot type*, and produces raised cast-metal type consisting of an alloy of lead, tin, and antimony known as type metal. Average machine speed is from about 3 characters per second (cps) for manual operation to about 20 cps for tape operation.

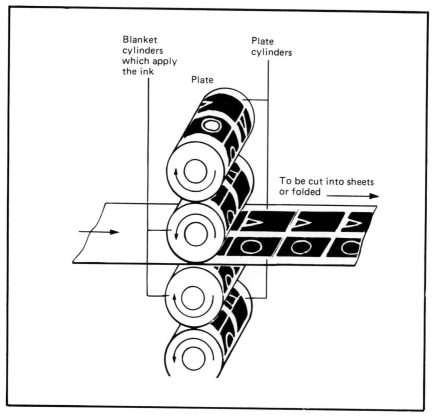

Fig. 1.6 Blanket-to-blanket printing unit. (We gratefully acknowledge International Paper Company's permission to use the illustrations appearing in its copyrighted publication, *POCKET PAL*® .)

Two other forms of typesetting in use are strike-on composition and photo-typesetting, sometimes called computersetting, because most phototypesetters use computers for various functions. Strike-on composition, or *cold type*, is produced on typewriters. Special typewriters are used with several typefaces, symbols, and spacing. Strike-on composition is more reasonable in cost than cast metal or phototypesetting, but the image quality of the composition is not as good. Quality has been improved on electronic typewriters used in word processing that interface with phototypesetters.

Phototypesetting is a means of producing type photographically, thereby shortening the number of production steps leading to the complete film master required in the platemaking for every major printing process. The first generation of phototypesetters was a line casting machine in which the metal matrix in the hot metal caster was replaced with an optical system for forming the characters on film or paper. Later generations of phototypesetters included equipment using computers for "justifying" lines and hyphenating words and cathode ray tubes for displaying characters at speeds exceeding 1,000 characters per second. Despite these developments, none of these machines could make headway against the hot metal casting machines until the video display terminal (VDT) was introduced in 1970. With the VDT, corrections can be made electronically without requiring manual manipulation of the copy, and type can be set at phenomenal speeds. Now electronic systems have been developed that compose complete pages, eliminating the labor-intensive operations of manual image assembly. Eventually typesetting will be eliminated as composed pages of text will be stored digitally in computer memory and interfaced with pictures and other image elements to produce completely imposed flats for platemaking.

Process photography

Process photography is the term used for the photographic techniques employed in the graphic arts process. Some platemaking processes require negatives and some positives. Some require correct reading on the plate, and others, reverse reading. The negatives or positives can be line, continuous tone, or halftone.

Any picture or scene consists of a number of different tones or gradations of tones known as *continuous tone*. In a photographic print, these are represented by varying amounts of silver in the print. The more silver, the darker the tone, and vice versa. In letterpress or lithography, these tones cannot be represented by varying amounts of ink with a single impression on the press. In order to produce the tones necessary to reproduce a picture, these processes must use the *halftone principle*. This is an optical illusion in which the tones are represented by solid dots that all have equal spacing and ink density but vary in area (Fig. 1.7). These dots are too small to be seen individually at the usual reading distance, but it is possible to see them by close examination of a halftone newspaper illustration or with a magnifying glass on finer screen rulings.

There are several nonscreen printing processes that can print varying densities of ink and use continuous tone negatives or positives, but they are difficult to work and not widely used. These include conventional gravure, screenless lithography, and collotype or photogelatin. Conventional gravure and screenless lithography are described later in this chapter. In collotype, the image consists of reticulated gelatin which prints ink directly in proportion to the amount of exposure received through a continuous tone negative.

Process photography is completed on large cameras with suspension systems to eliminate the effects of vibration on the images, since long exposures are used in comparison with amateur or commercial photography

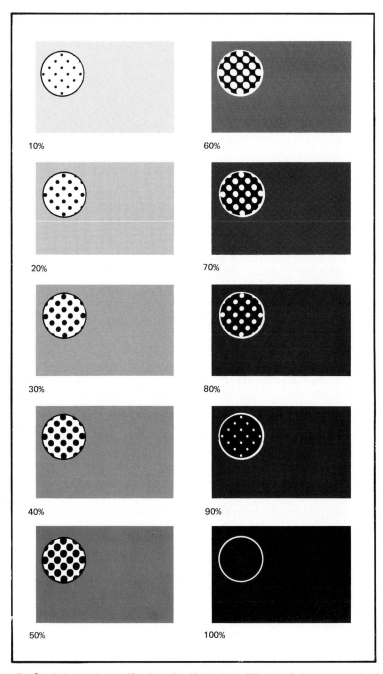

Fig. 1.7 Gradation and magnification of halftone dots. (We gratefully acknowledge International Paper Company's permission to use the illustrations appearing in its copyright publication, *POCKET PAL®* .)

(Fig. 1.8). Cameras can be either horizontal or vertical. Horizontal types have bed or overhead suspension. Most process cameras have a copy board, lens, and bellows in the camera room, and a camera back built into the darkroom wall. Enlargers are also used, especially for making color separations for color reproduction.

Fig. 1.8   Floor-type horizontal camera. (We gratefully acknowledge International Paper Company's permission to use the illustrations appearing in its copyrighted publication, *POCKET PAL®* .)

Lenses for process work are coated to reduce flare and are usually of symmetrical design to eliminate distortion in the images. Because of the requirements for high resolution and minimum aberrations, process lenses have fairly small maximum apertures—from F/8 to F/11. Focal lengths range from 8 in. for wide angle lenses for 20-in. cameras to as long as 48 in. for a 40-in. camera. Some cameras use prisms for reversing the image laterally, as is required for photoengraving.

The films used consist of special high contrast, orthochromatic emulsions of silver halides in gelatin on a stable film base for line and halftone photography, continuous tone orthochromatic film for gravure, and continuous tone panchromatic film for color separations and masks. Special developers are used for high contrast. An important and significant trend in recent years has been the increased use of automatic processing machines which are capable of developing, fixing, washing, and drying film in less time and with less variation than hand processing.

Line photography

Line copy consists of solids, line drawings, and text matter. In photography, the copy is placed on the copyboard of the camera, illuminated by high intensity lights, and focused to the correct size on a ground glass in the back of the camera. The film is placed on the vacuum back of the camera which is put in place of the ground glass. The aperture is set on the lens, and the exposure is made through a solenoid shutter operated manually using a stopwatch, or automatically by a timer or a light integrating meter. The film is then developed, fixed, and washed either in trays or in an automatic processor. This operation produces a high contrast negative which is reverse reading on the emulsion side.

Halftone photography

Halftones are produced mainly two ways: using a glass crossline screen or using a contact screen. The crossline screen consists of two sheets of glass, each ruled with parallel lines which are approximately equal in width to the spaces between them, cemented together at right angles to each other. The screen ruling is the number of lines per inch. Newspapers printed by letterpress commonly use screens with rulings of 65–80 lines per inch, while those printed by offset lithography employ screens with rulings from 80–120 lines per inch. For magazines and commercial printing by both letterpress and offset lithography, screen rulings normally are between 133–150 lines per inch. A 133-line screen halftone is just beyond the resolving power of the eye at normal reading distance. Screens with finer rulings are generally used only for printing color and on coated papers.

As a general rule, the finer the screen ruling, the sharper the rendition of detail in the reproduction. Usually there is little advantage, however, in using a screen finer than 150 lines per inch for a black and white or a single color reproduction because there is a minimum dot size printed in the highlights of the reproduction; with finer screens, the step from the white of the paper to the first printed dot is too great, and tone reproduction in the highlight suffers. In color reproduction, the finer the screen, the purer the color: more of the image is covered with ink and the graying effect of white paper is reduced.

Photography with a crossline screen involves placing the screen in the back of the camera in a special screen holder that can be moved precisely a very short distance from the film. During exposure, each opening in the screen acts like a pinhole and produces patterns on the film which result in dots proportional in size to the amount of light reflected from the corresponding area of the copy (Fig. 1.9). The lighter the area of the copy, the more light is reflected, which results in larger patterns and larger dots. The darker areas reflect less light, producing smaller patterns, so the dots are smaller. All dots have the same spacing, but vary in area, as shown in Fig. 1.7.

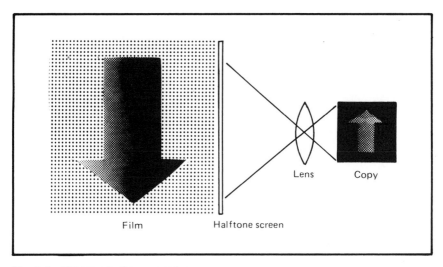

Fig. 1.9 Making a halftone negative.

Contact screens are now more widely used than the crossline screen. The contact screen is on film base and is made from a glass screen. It consists of vignetted dot elements with variable density across each dot, all with equal spacing corresponding to the ruling of the glass screen from which it is made (Fig. 1.10). There are gray screens in which the dots consist of the silver images developed in the screen after exposure, development, and fixing. There are also dyed screens, usually magenta. Special screens such as the chain dot screen, which has elliptical dots, and the Respi screen, which has highlight dots that have double the spacing of the middletone and shadow dots are also used.

Photography with a contact screen is much simpler and requires much less skill than photography with a glass screen. The screen is placed in contact with the film. Because of the variable density across each vignetted dot in the screen, the dots on the film in contact with the screen vary in size according to the amount of light reflected from the copy. The contrast of reproduction can be varied within limits by techniques known as *flashing* and *no-screen bump exposures*. With dyed screens there is additional control of contrast by using different colored filters during part of the exposure.

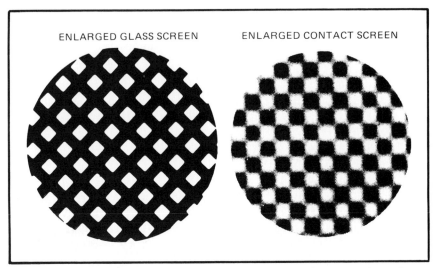

Fig. 1.10 Making a contact screen. (We gratefully acknowledge International Paper Company's permission to use the illustrations appearing in its copyright publication, *POCKET PAL®* .)

Tone reproduction and contrast are two important conditions that determine the quality of the reproduction. If a stepped gray scale is used, good tone reproduction in halftone photography is achieved when the darkest area of the subject (shadow) prints as a solid on the press sheet and the lightest area (highlight) prints as a white with no evidence of a screen in either tone. The intermediate tones of the gray scale should have varying sizes of dots from about a 2–5% dot area in the highlight end to about an 80–95% dot area in the shadows with a checkerboard pattern in the 50% middletone area. The minimum printable dot sizes depend on the conditions of printing and whether the printing is on smooth or rough papers, with coated paper giving the longest scale and range of dot sizes when printed properly.

In both glass and contact screen photography, contrast can be increased or decreased deliberately. *High contrast* exists when two or three steps in the shadow end print solid and/or several steps in the highlight end print white with a corresponding increase in density difference or *gamma* between the other steps of the scale. When the deepest blacks contain 80–90% dot area and/or the highlights a 10–20% dot area with reduced density differences in the rest of the scale, the reproduction has *low contrast*.

Color reproduction

Color reproduction is based on the theory of three-color vision. In this theory, white light, which contains all the wavelengths of light, consists of three primary colors: blue, green, and red. These are broad bands of color as distinguished from the physical concept of color in which each wavelength of light varies in color from every other wavelength. The eye contains three different types of receptors in the cones on the retina, each sensitive to one of the primary colors of light. When the eye views a scene, the receptors in the cones are activated by the colors they are sensitive to and send impulses to the brain. The brain recreates the scene from the impulses it receives. The fidelity of the scene recreated by the brain depends on the experience of the viewer and the condition of the receptors. If any of these is diseased or sensitivity is impaired, color blindness results, and the visual impression of color is distorted.

Color separation. The process of color separation in color reproduction is similar to the way the eye sees color. Blue, green, and red are called additive primaries because three lights of these colors add together to produce white light. Whenever white light is seen by the eye, it is a combination of blue, green, and red light. The many different shades of whites are the result of changes in the amounts of blue, green, and red light reflected to the eye.

In color separation photography, the subject is photographed using three filters, each corresponding in color and light transmission to one of the additive primaries. When the subject is photographed with the red filter over the lens, the negative produced is the red separation negative: this is a recording of all the red light reflected from, or, in the case of a transparency, transmitted through the subject. When a positive is made from this negative, the image in this positive corresponds to the areas in the subject which do not contain red, or contain the other two colors of light, namely, blue and green. In effect, the negative has subtracted the red light from the subject, and the positive is a recording of the two remaining colors, blue and green. This combination of color is called *cyan*, and the positive is called the cyan printer.

Photography through the green filter produces the green separation negative which records the green in the subject. The positive made from this negative is a recording of the red and blue, called *magenta*; the positive is called the magenta printer.

Photography through the blue filter produces the blue separation negative which records the blue in the subject. The positive made from this negative is a recording of the red and green, which when lights of these colors are combined is called *yellow*; the positive is called the yellow printer.

Magenta, yellow, and cyan are subtractive primaries: colors which are left after one additive primary is subtracted from white light. These are the colors which are used for the printing inks in process color reproduction.

Ideal vs. actual pigments. When the positive made from the blue separation printed in yellow ink is combined with the positive from the green separation negative printed in magenta ink, and the positive from the red separation negative printed in cyan ink, the result *should* be a faithful reproduction of the original. Actually, it is not. The colors except yellow and red are dirty and muddied. There is too much yellow in the reds and greens, and too much red in the blues and purples. This is not because the theory is at fault, but because the pigments used in the inks for color reproduction are not ideal.

The yellow pigments used for color reproduction are quite good in spectral characteristics, but not so with the magentas and cyans. The ideal yellow pigment, when illuminated with white light, should reflect all the green and red light, and absorb all the blue light. The yellows used absorb most of the blue light, reflect practically all of the red light, and absorb a small amount of the green light; the yellows are very slightly orange.

The ideal magenta should reflect all the blue and red light and absorb all the green light when illuminated with white light. Actual magentas reflect a small amount of green light, absorb some red light and appreciable blue light so that they are slightly gray (green reflectance) and behave as though they have considerable yellow (blue absorption) in them.

The ideal cyan, when illuminated with white light, should reflect all the blue and green light, and absorb all the red light. Actual cyans reflect some red light and absorb considerable blue and green light. They are reddish, (red reflectance) quite gray or dirty (blue absorption), and behave as though they have considerable yellow (blue absorption) and magenta (green absorption) in them. The inaccuracies of the inks can be determined by making densitometer readings of the inks using filters corresponding to the additive primaries or the filters used for color separations.

Due to color deficiencies in the pigments used in process color printing inks, corrections must be made in the color separation negatives or positives to compensate for the inks' color deficiencies and for their effect on the final reproduction. The amount of yellow printing with the magenta and cyan printers must be reduced to compensate for the excess blue absorption of these inks, and the amount of magenta printing with the cyan printer must be reduced to counterbalance the excess green absorption of cyan inks. In correcting color reproduction errors, color, ink absorption, and gloss of the paper also must be considered since they affect the hue, grayness, and saturation of the inks.

Even after corrections are made, a reproduction made from the three corrected printers printed with the proper inks would still not be satisfactory. The deep shadows would be brownish instead of neutral because of the poor blue reflectance of the magenta ink and especially the low blue and green reflectance of the cyan ink and they lack contrast. To overcome this, a fourth printer, black, is used. This is the basis for four-color process printing. The black is used to make the deep shadows neutral and increase their contrast.

The black printer can be a skeleton black or a full black, depending on the process used or type of printing done. Most offset lithography is done with a skeleton black. Most letterpress, especially high-speed magazine printing, is done with a relatively full black, and the other colors are proportionately reduced in these areas so that the inks transfer or "trap" properly on the high-speed presses. Gravure also uses full black printers. Reducing the colors and printing a full black in the shadow areas is called *undercolor removal.*

Color correction

Spectral errors in the inks may be corrected manually, photographically, or electronically. Manually, corrections usually are made on the halftone positives made from the color separation negatives by *dot-etching*: reducing the sizes of the dots with chemical reducers. Manual corrections on the metal halftone plates used for letterpress printing or on the cylinders used for gravure printing are completed by etching the dots locally after the plates or cylinders are made. This operation is called *fine etching* or *re-etching.*

When color corrections are done photographically, the operation is called *masking*. In this operation, a positive of one separation negative is placed over another separation negative to reduce ink density in unwanted areas.

Electronic scanning can also be used for color correction. The original, usually a transparency or color print which can be wrapped around a drum, is scanned with a light beam that is transmitted or reflected and split into three beams, each beam going to a photocell covered with a red, green, or blue filter (Fig. 1.11). These separate the copy into its three color components. The electrical signals from the photocell are fed into four separate computers, one for each color, and one for the black which is computed from the other three signals. The computers can be preset to modify the currents depending on the inks, paper, tonal range, undercolor removal, and other printing conditions. The modified currents are fed to exposing lights which vary in intensity in proportion to the corrected value of each element in the area scanned. Fig. 1.11 shows an instrument which produces four separations simultaneously. Other scanners produce one or two separations at a time. Most of the newer scanners in use produce screened negative or positive color separations directly using contact screens or electronic dot generators with lasers for producing the halftones.

With the development of low cost mini- and micro-computers and suitable software, electronic scanners have been programmed so that they produce not only color corrected separations, but also produce them at correct size and in the correct position on a page. Considerable handwork in positioning color separation films accurately in page layouts is eliminated and cost savings achieved. A number of systems have been developed to accomplish page composition of color elements with a single color text, diagrams, and other illustrations.

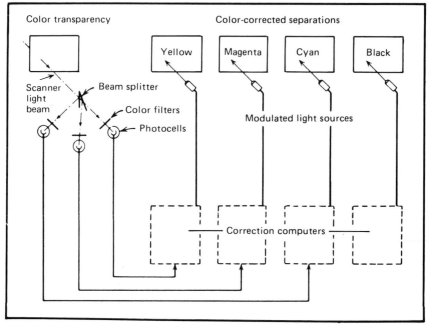

Fig. 1.11 Electronic scanner. (We gratefully acknowledge International Paper Company's permission to use the illustrations appearing in its copyright publication, *POCKET PAL®* .)

Screen angles

In four-color process printing from halftones, there is a problem with patterns from the screen angles. The patterns are called *moiré*, and are caused by the superposition of the halftone screens. With the screen rulings commonly used, a minimum pattern is formed when the axes of the screens are separated by 30°. Since halftone screens consist of rulings at 90° to each other, there is room for only three 30° angles before they repeat. In four-color printing, two of the colors must be printed either at the same angle or separated by other than 30°. The usual screen angles are yellow 0°, cyan 15°, black 45°, and magenta 75°. These angles can cause moiré patterns in greens and reds and can be changed. The further two colors are apart, the less the moiré pattern appears. The angles themselves are also very critical. Errors as small as 0.1° can cause objectionable moiré patterns in grays or areas where three and four colors print together. Both slight misregister between colors or local distortion of the paper in printing and improper transfer of ink, called poor trapping, can cause moiré patterns. Electronic screening in some electronic scanning systems cannot produce angles of 30° between colors. They use angles of about 18° and 72° for two of the colors and try to compensate for moiré by changing the screen rulings between colors from 150-line to approximately 200-line screen.

Ink trapping

Proper trapping results when the same amount of ink transfers to a previously inked area of the paper as to an unprinted area. Poor trapping results when less ink transfers to the inked area than to blank paper. This is a serious problem in printing on high-speed multicolor presses on which ink must transfer to wet ink films. It is much more serious in letterpress than in off-set, as thicker ink films are printed. If the inks are not formulated to trap properly, poor trapping results, which shows up as weak overprint colors (red, green, and blue) and accentuated moiré patterns. Gravure often shows effects of overtrapping, as the inks are dried between printings and there is more holdout of ink printed over dried ink than on plain paper. Ink absorption of paper can have a serious effect on trapping.

Image assembly

After the films are completed for a job, they must be opaqued to remove pinholes and other defects; outlined, cut apart, or cut to size; and assembled onto a form according to a specific layout for exposing onto a plate. This is a tedious, time-consuming, and labor-intensive job and often the most serious bottleneck in production.

The arranging of pages in a form for printing in the proper sequence or in position after the sheet is cut, folded, and trimmed is called image assembly, or *stripping*, in lithography and other forms of photomechanical platemaking. The unit produced is known as a *signature*. There are three basic types of imposition for signatures: sheetwise, work-and-turn, and work-and-tumble. In sheetwise imposition, different pages are printed on each side of the sheet. It is used if the run is long and the number of pages is large enough to fill the full capacity of the plate.

In both work-and-turn and work-and-tumble imposition, all the pages for both sides of the sheet are printed on the same form, which produces two finished units to the sheet. In work-and-turn, once the first side is printed, the sheet is turned over from left to right and the second side is printed. The same gripper edge but a different side guide is used for printing the two sides; thus, squareness of the sheets is important. In work-and-tumble, once the first side is printed, the sheet is turned over from gripper edge to back for the printing of the second side. Changing the gripper edge and side guide can cause problems in register if the paper has bowed edges and is not accurately sized, squared, and trimmed.

In stripping for photomechanical plates, the imposition is done on a flat with film taped into position on a sheet of colored masking (goldenrod) paper or on special orange plastic sheets if color or close register is involved. When all the film is in place, the stripper cuts windows out from the masking sheet, permitting light to pass through the film during exposure to the plate. The stripper also puts together all elements of a page if they are in separate pieces. If positives are needed for the platemaking process, a contact film is made of the flat.

When a large printing is required of a relatively small label or package, press time is saved by combining a number of duplicate negatives or positives on a plate. This is done ordinarily with a step-and-repeat machine, which produces multiple images of negatives or positives on a printing plate according to a predetermined layout. It consists of a bed for mounting the plate, a chase for mounting the film, means for traversing the chase accurately in the X and Y directions, a high intensity lamp like pulsed Xenon or metal halide for exposure, and an integrating device for controlling exposure.

Automated imposition

The three different systems for automatically positioning pages on a plate to eliminate manual operations of stripping are automated step and repeat, optical imposition, and microstripping.

Some step-and-repeat machines have devices for advancing the chase in the X and Y directions automatically using programmed punched tape, punched cards, or keyboard input. Some are also equipped with special programmed film cassettes that operate completely automatically by rejecting one film after all the exposures with that film have been completed, and picking up the next film for continuing the exposures on the plate. Automatic step and repeat machines are useful in packaging and in book production where the negatives are programmed in advance for exposure in the proper position on the plate. Pin register is used extensively both in stripping and in step and repeat.

One type of equipment for optical imposition or projection stripping consists of a precision process camera that exposes all subjects on the optical axis of the lens. The camera has a movable back which automatically and accurately positions each exposure in its correct X, Y positions according to a computer program for the signature being imposed. This system is used in plants printing books, publications, labels, and other specialties.

There are two systems in limited use for microstripping in which original pages, usually text, are reduced in size to 35 mm or 70 mm films, processed, examined, stored, and reprojected to original size on a plate using special projectors and computer programs to position the pages correctly on the plates. These systems are responsible for appreciable savings in film costs, but they are in limited use because conventional plates require special projectors with quartz optics which are not only expensive, but also have limited corrections: halftones do not reproject well. Newly developed high-speed plates will make these systems more practical and cost effective.

There are also computerized layout systems using CAD/CAM techniques that produce film of opaque-cut film layouts with blank areas corresponding to positions where type, line drawings, and halftone films are mounted.

Platemaking

As mentioned, each printing process uses a plate, or some form of image carrier, to transfer the image to the paper during printing. With the exception of handmade stencils for screen printing, some steel die engraving, and hand and machine set cast metal type for letterpress, most image carriers are made by photomechanical means. The plates used for letterpress and flexographic printing are made by photoengraving or photopolymer processes. Most plates used for lithographic printing are presensitized and can be surface, deep etch, or bi-metal, depending on the length of the press run. Gravure plates or cylinders can be conventional, direct transfer, or variable area–variable depth.

Photomechanical plates use light sensitive materials or coatings which change in physical properties after exposure to light. Most of the materials in use change in solubility in water or other solutions: the unexposed areas dissolve and leave the exposed portions to serve as the image or a stencil, or resist, for forming the image. The types of coatings in use include bichromated colloids, which are used for some gravure, engraving, and lithographic plates, and are being phased out because of the toxicity of the bichromates; diazos, which are used extensively in lithography; and photopolymers, which are used in engraving and lithography. Silver halide and electrostatic coatings are also used in duplicating.

Photoengraving

The plates used for letterpress printing are original, duplicate, or wraparound. Original engravings are made on zinc, magnesium, or copper of about 16 gauge or 0.065 in. (1.65 mm) in thickness. The most common method used for making metal engravings is powderless etching. Duplicate plates are used for long runs, and are plastic for some newspaper and specialty printing, rubber for flexography, stereotypes for newspaper printing, and electrotypes for magazine and quality commercial printing. Most original and duplicate plates are made in small pieces or page sizes for assembly on to a form or the printing cylinder of the press.

Wraparound plates are made in one piece to be wrapped around the plate cylinder of the press. All copy is in the proper position for printing, reducing the time for makeready. Wraparound plates for letterpress are plastic or metal in shallow relief, with thicknesses from 0.017 in. (0.043 mm) to 0.030 in. (0.76 mm); they bend to fit into the cylinder clamps and conform to the cylinder during printing. Most wraparound plates are used for lithography, but are also used for offset letterpress or letterpress printing; gravure plates are used for sheet-fed gravure.

Photopolymer plates are precoated and can be used as original or direct and wraparound plates. Many photopolymer plates have been developed for newspaper and flexographic printing. At present, a plate on a steel base and mounted on magnetic cylinders is the most popular plate used in letterpress.

Gravure plate and cylinder making

Most modern gravure printing is completed on web presses from images etched in copper plated cylinders, and is generally referred to as *rotogravure*. These cylinders can vary from 3 in. (76 mm) in diameter by 1 in. (25 mm) wide for printing special labels to 17 or 18 ft (5.2 or 5.5 m) wide by 3 ft (0.9 m) in diameter for printing floor coverings. Magazine presses range from 6 to over 8 ft wide (1.8 to over 2.4 m). On sheet-fed presses, the printing element is usually a thin copper plate wrapped around the cylinder. Preparation of the printing surface is essentially the same for both cylinders and plates.

Three different types of plate and cylinder making systems used for gravure are: conventional, where all the elements are the same size, but vary in depth, giving a long scale of reproduction used for high quality printing of photographs; direct transfer or variable area, used mainly for packaging; variable area–variable depth, used extensively for magazine and catalog printing.

One serious problem with gravure cylinder making has been the difficulty in reproducing cylinders from the same originals. Differences in materials, etching solutions, impurities in the copper, environmental conditions, and other factors affecting chemical etching are contributing factors to the problem. Different methods have been developed as an attempt to control the tone reproduction of gravure cylinders: controlled etching, powderless etching, and electromechanical engraving. Research continues with lasers and with electron beam etching.

Lithographic platemaking

Lithography was first produced on stone about 1800 by Senefelder. Metal replaced stone about 1900. On a lithographic plate, the separation between image and nonimage areas which are essentially on the same plane must be maintained chemically by the principle that grease and water do not mix. The image areas on a lithographic plate must be ink receptive and refuse water. The nonimage areas must be water receptive and refuse ink. To a small extent, grease and water do mix; this is an essential element for successful lithography. Maintaining a wide difference between ink receptivity of the image areas and water receptivity of the nonimage areas results in a better plate, an easier press run, and consistent quality prints.

Ink receptivity is achieved using inherently oleophilic (oil-loving) photosensitive resins such as diazos, polymers, or lacquers and metals like copper or brass. Water receptivity of the nonimage areas is achieved by using inherently hydrophilic (water-loving) metals such as aluminum, chromium, or stainless steel and treating them with silicate and/or phosphate ions in platemaking. Properly treated anodized aluminum has especially good water receptivity in addition to good wear characteristics on the press. Fountain solutions on the press are important for maintaining water receptivity of the plates during printing.

Water receptivity is maintained in platemaking and printing by natural and synthetic gums. The most widely used gum is gum arabic. Synthetic gums more consistent in properties than natural gums presently used are now produced. The gums are modified in a dilute solution with phosphate, nitrate, and bichromate ions, and are maintained at a pH value of about 2.0 as a plate desensitizer or "etch" and at a pH value of between 4.5 and 5.0 as a fountain etch for dampening the plates on the press.

Lithographic plates are classified as surface, deep-etch, and bi-metal. Surface plates are those in which the light sensitive coating eventually becomes the ink-receptive image area on the plate. This is the most popular type of plate, represented by the diazo and the photopolymer plates. Most of these plates are presensitized. A number of wipe-on surface plates are used for shorter runs and newspaper printing. On deep-etch plates, the coating is removed from the image areas, and then chemically coppered and/or lacquered and inked so they are ink receptive. These are used for long runs of color printing and packaging. Bi-metal plates are similar to deep-etch plates in that the coating is removed from the image areas, but these areas consist of copper or brass, either as a base metal or copper electroplated on another metal and the nonimage areas are aluminum, stainless steel, or chromium. Bi-metal plates are used for very long runs in packaging and on web presses.

Lithographic plates are easy to correct and less expensive than other plates. Images can be readily added or deleted on all types of plates without extensive and intricate hand tooling, which is required on letterpress plates and gravure cylinders. Also, automatic processors exist for every platemaking process or plate.

Handling lithographic plates on the press. Bi-metal plates are the easiest plates to run on the press because they are almost indestructible. If anything happens to the plate on the press, it can be fixed relatively easily; a single treatment usually restores the plate to its proper printing condition. With other types of lithographic plates, the treatments used on the press to help one area are generally injurious to the other area. Treatments to make the image more ink receptive are apt to cause the nonimage areas to scum if the pressman is not careful. Treatments designed to make the nonimage areas water receptive are inclined to blind the image areas. Extreme care must be used with these treatments. Often it is more economical to make new plates.

Plate life is generally about twice as long on web offset presses as on sheet-fed presses with the same papers and inks. The reasons are obvious: the large gaps on the sheet-fed plate and the blanket cylinders interrupt the ink-water cycle, which necessitates more adjustment of the ink-water settings, resulting in premature wear of the image and nonimage areas of the plate. On a web press, however, the ink and water are in better dynamic balance due to the very small gap, which results in less damage to the plate, hence, longer run length. When comparing plate run lengths, the difference between printing on web- and sheet-fed presses can vary by as much as a factor of two.

New plate developments

An important new development in lithographic platemaking is the use of baking ovens to extend the press wear resistance of photopolymer coatings on lithographic plates. Run life on these plates has been increased to a million impressions or more on web offset presses.

In 1970, a new process of platemaking known as driography was introduced by 3M. The image areas on the plates are inks on metal and the nonimage areas are silicone rubber which has no affinity for ink, so no water is needed in printing. Because of problems with toning of the nonprinting areas, 3M phased out its production of driographic plates in 1977. Toray, a Japanese firm, however, has produced some excellent reproductions, and the process is in extended field testing and limited commercial use. The potential of driography for simplifying the production of quality printing with minimum waste is greater than any of the printing processes, including flexography. Its use, however, may create paper problems due to the use of inks with rheological properties and the absence of water.

Considerable effort is being expended to produce printing plates with the speed and spectral sensitivity required for projection and laser platemakers. None has been completely successful. The most promising to date are new electrostatic printing plates with exposure speeds comparable with lithifilm, so they can be used in projection platemaking systems under conditions similar to exposing on films and in laser platemaking using low cost, high reliability He/Cd lasers.

There are two commercial laser platemakers for making lithographic plates with lasers, primarily for newspapers. One system uses two lasers: a He/Ne laser to scan a pasteup of the copy for a newspaper page, and an Argon ion laser to expose a regular plate, usually a diazo wipe-on. Another system also uses two lasers: a He/Ne laser to scan a pasteup page and a YAG laser to expose an intermediate Lasermask in contact with an aluminum plate. During exposure, the Lasermask, which is coated with a special black coating, releases the coating in the areas exposed by the YAG laser and these areas transfer to the plate, forming the image of the printing plate. The Lasermask becomes a negative which can be used to expose duplicate plates. With proper software, both systems can be used to produce plates directly from digitized information in a computer.

Because of problems with water pollution caused by platemaking developing chemicals, a number of water developable plates have been produced for lithographic printing. Some firms have developed higher speed plates than conventional diazo and photopolymer plates for projection and laser platemakers, but these plates are still one to two orders of speed too slow for practical use.

Screens for screen printing

There are many methods for making screens for screen printing. As already mentioned, the screen is porous, and the image is produced by blocking the pores in the screen in the nonprinting areas. This can be done manually by cutting out templates and adhering them to the screen; photomechanically by coating the screen with a sensitizer, exposing a positive so the nonprinting areas are hardened, blocking the screen, and the image areas develop so the ink penetrates the screen; or by using a material like carbon tissue, or special transfer film as used in gravure and transferring these to the screen instead of the copper cylinder, and then washing out the unexposed areas which represent the image.

The latest method of screen printing is a rotary screen, which is made by plating the cylinder electrolytically on a steel cylinder, removing the plated cylinder, applying a photomechanical coating to it, exposing it through a positive and a screen, and etching out the image areas to form pores in the cylinders. On rotary screen presses, the ink is pumped into the cylinder and the squeegee is also inside the cylinder.

Electrophotographic plates

For duplicating or reprography, some printing systems use plates made by electrophotographic means. One method uses a selenium plate or drum; another method uses the electrofax principle in which zinc oxide is dispersed in a binder and coated on paper or metal; a third method uses an organic photoconductor.

In all these methods, the plate or drum is charged with a corona discharge and exposed in a camera to produce the printing image. Toner is applied to the exposed plate and in the case of selenium, after development the image is transferred to a paper or metal plate. The toner on the image is fixed by heat or solvent vapor and in the case of an electrofax plate, the nonimage area is treated with a special fountain solution which contains ferrocyanide to make it water receptive. In the third method, the organic photoconductor is dissolved from the nonprinting areas and printing is done from the toned photoconductor in the image areas.

Other plates for reprography

Direct image plates can be prepared by typing, drawing, or lettering directly onto a paper master. Special ribbons, pencils, and inks are used. Although inexpensive and easy to make, these plates are limited in quality and are used only for short runs. Two types of silver emulsion plates are used for reprography. In one type, the plate is made directly in the camera, processed, and mounted on the press. Different grades of plates are made for runs up to 5,000. The other consists of two photographic emulsions coated on a paper base which, after exposure and development, produce areas corresponding to the image which are ink receptive while the nonimage areas remain water receptive. The plate has a rather sensitive ink-water balance, but it has produced runs in excess of 10,000 impressions. A number of plates for reprography use the diffusion transfer principle, which is similar to the principle of Polaroid film. The two-part system consists of a negative material on which the exposure is made, and a receiver material to which the image is transferred and becomes the printing plate.

Printing

The second part of the printing process is printing and finishing, specialized operations which are as related to the cost and quality of the final product, if not more so, than the preparatory operations. Press time is the most expensive operating cost item in a printing plant. The more that can be done in the preparatory operations—in photography, to make sure the type and tone values are correct, and in platemaking, to make sure the images are in correct position, the proper plate is selected and is treated, or *madeready*, to print properly—the less down time there will be on the press, resulting in improved production and a higher return on investment. More press and finishing operations are becoming automated, which places even more emphasis on speeding up, and reducing the cost of the preparatory operations.

Printing is handled by presses which contain means for mounting plates or image carriers on a bed or cylinder (or in the case of rotogravure for mounting the actual printing cylinder); devices for inking the plates; means for feeding the paper and adjusting the tension on web presses; arrangements for transferring the inked image to the paper; and means for delivering the printed matter as sheets in a pile, as folded signatures in a stack, or rewinding in a roll.

Presses are either sheet-fed or roll- (web) fed. Commercial printing traditionally has been handled on sheet-fed presses, but lately much of it is being done on web presses, especially by lithography. Presses can be single color or multicolor, where a number of colors in succession are printed. Usually on a multicolor press, each color requires a separate complete printing unit: inking, plate, and impression mechanism. In gravure, each unit has a dryer; on blanket-to-blanket web offset presses, the blanket of one unit serves as the impression cylinder of the opposing unit. A two-color press would have two units, a four-color press would have four, etc., in tandem or around a common impression cylinder. In packaging and other special-purpose equipment, it is common to have presses with combinations of lithographic, letterpress and/or gravure units.

Letterpress printing

Letterpress is the oldest of the printing processes with the widest variety of printing equipment. While some of the methods are now considered obsolete, they are still used in job shops and private presses. The three types of letterpress presses are platen, flat bed cylinder, and rotary.

Platen presses were used by Gutenberg to print his famous Bible. They have two flat surfaces, the bed and the platen. Cast metal type and photoengraved plates can be mounted and locked in position on the bed. The type and plates are inked by inking rollers, and the impression is made or, "pulled" on sheets fed manually or automatically on the platen. They are still used for many different purposes such as job printing on paper and paperboard, envelopes, imprinting, embossing, steel-rule die-cutting, and hot roll and goldleaf die stamping.

Flat-bed cylinder presses are made with horizontal and vertical beds. They also can print cast metal type and photoengraved plates, but the sheets feed automatically over a cylinder. The horizontal presses print larger sheets than the platen presses. Three types of horizontal presses are single color, two-color, and perfecting, on which both sides of the sheet are printed in one pass through the press, the sheet being turned over between impressions. The presses are slow and much of the work formerly done on these presses has been converted to rotary presses or lithography. Their manufacture was discontinued in the U.S. in 1962, but some are still being manufactured in Europe.

The vertical flat-bed cylinder presses are popular job presses with automatic inking and feeding. They are used in many printing plants for general job and commercial printing and imprinting.

The greatest amount of letterpress is printed on rotary presses, including long-run commercial work, packaging, newspapers, and magazines. Sheet-fed presses were made in sizes up to 54.5 × 77 in. (1384 × 1956 mm) with rated speeds as high as 6,000 iph, but the manufacture of large rotary presses has been discontinued due to decreased demand. Plates must be curved for mounting on rotary presses. Stereos, electros, molded plastic or rubber, photopolymer, and wraparound plates can be used. One type of wraparound press was built like an offset press with three equal size cylinders. The plate is mounted on normally the blanket cylinder and the plate cylinder is used as an inking drum for even distribution.

Web-fed rotary letterpress presses are of many sizes and styles and are used for periodical, book, and newspaper printing. Two types are used for periodical and book printing: the unit type, which has a separate complete printing unit for each color, and the common impression cylinder type, often called the "satellite" type, on which the printing units are situated around a large cylinder which serves as the impression cylinder for all the plate cylinders. The unit type has the advantage of allowing more time between impressions so ink trapping is better. The common impression cylinder type has the advantage of better register since the sheet is held firmly over the impression cylinder between impressions. Since much periodical and book printing is done on coated paper, these presses are equipped with dryers, usually of the hot air, high velocity type. The use of dryers entails the use of heat set inks, which in turn require the use of chill rollers to cool and set the resins in the inks after they have been softened going through the dryer.

Letterpress newspaper presses are web-fed rotary presses which are built in couples with each couple printing both sides of the paper in succession, usually 16 pages, 8 pages on each side. This is known as the 4-page wide press. The latest in letterpress newspaper presses is the 6-page wide press which is 90 in. (2286 mm) wide and prints 12 pages on each side. Because of the use of highly absorptive papers, dryers are not used on letterpress newspaper presses. Many letterpress newspaper presses are being converted to offset lithographic presses by the installation of special conversion units.

Flexographic presses are also rotary web-fed letterpress presses which are used mainly in packaging. The three types of flexographic presses are stack type, in which two or three printing units are placed vertically in stacks and a complete press can consist of two or three stacks, with unwind, rewind, sheeter or cutter and creaser; central impression cylinder, similar to common impression cylinder magazine press, which is used extensively for printing lightweight papers and flexible films; in-line, which is similar to the unit type magazine press.

Flexography uses rubber plates and water- or solvent-based inks in simple two roller inking systems. It is one of the least expensive and simplest of the printing processes, and has been used for decorating inexpensive packaging. Quality was not an object, but recently good quality printing has been achieved on paper and flexible films using precision photopolymer plates and special inking systems, some equipped with ceramic rollers and some with reverse angle doctor blades. A doctor blade is placed in the opposite direction of travel of the inking roller known as the anilox roller. Usually, hot air velocity dryers are used on these presses to drive off the solvents and dry the inks. Some book presses for printing low cost books like paperbacks without halftone illustrations use rubber plates and essentially the flexographic process. Flexographic presses are also being developed and used for printing newspapers.

Some book presses print in-line: a complete book is printed in one pass through the press. The Cameron press, for example, has all the plates representing both sides of the pages on two flexible belts that print on the two sides of the paper web and the web is then slit into ribbons cut into 4-page signatures, collated into complete books, and then fed onto an automatic bindery line with preprinted covers feeding from another line. The results: a bound finished book, either hard or soft bound. Other in-line printers are similar, except that the plates for the two sides of the pages are mounted on different sized cylinders to accommodate different sized books.

One of the serious problems in letterpress printing is the variable pressure exerted by the different sized image elements in printing. The amount of printing pressure, or *squeeze*, which is needed for ink transfer, exerts more pressure on the small highlight dots or fine lines and serifs than on the larger shadow dots or larger image elements. This necessitates considerable makeready to even out the impression so that the highlights and fine lines print correctly and do not puncture the paper. Precision electrotypes, wraparound plates, and premakeready systems have helped reduce makeready time, but it is absolutely necessary for quality printing and is a reason letterpress has been replaced by other processes for some types of work.

In flexography and rubberplate book printing, the rubberplate distorts and compresses so that makeready is not so critical, and the process is easier. Because of the distortion, there is a limitation to the fineness of the screen image that can be printed and the register that can be maintained, especially on stack and unit type presses. With reasonable care, 150 line screen images have been printed on paper and flexible films with acceptable quality on central impression cylinder presses, using reverse angle doctor blades on the anilox rollers.

Tension is an important factor in web letterpress and web offset printing because relatively tacky inks are run in comparison with the fluid inks used on gravure and flexographic presses. Paper is drawn through a web press, creating a force known as web tension. It is important to control tension on a web press because of the variable nature of paper. Applying even a relatively small force to paper causes it to change dimensions, and the changes are not constant for a given paper, or even within a single roll. The erratic

Table 1.1 Advantages and limitations of letterpress printing

Advantages	Limitations
A simple process.	High cost of engravings.
Can print from metal type.	A direct transfer process.
Uses a variety of presses.	A relief process.
Prints with ink mass-tone.	Ink trapping on multicolor presses.
Good color uniformity throughout run.	Needs very smooth surfaces or mottle will result.
The separation between image and nonimage areas is mechanical.	Differential pressure requires time-consuming makeready.
Gloss inks and gold inks print well.	Problems with poor trapping due to thick ink films.

behavior of paper under stress usually results in inconsistencies in the final product such as variation in unit-to-unit register, side lay, cut-off, and folding accuracy. In extreme cases, the result is web breaks. To keep paper behavior uniform through the press, constant torque devices like a *dancer roll* or variable speed devices which control the flow rate of the web through the press are employed. Refer to Table 1.1 for a quick overview of letterpress printing advantages and limitations.

Gravure printing

Little gravure is printed from sheet-fed presses that use plates. The greatest amount of gravure is printed from cylinders on rolls of paper or film. The cylinders are removable and can have different diameters so that different print lengths can be accommodated from job to job. This is desirable in packaging, but unnecessary in most magazine printing. The gravure printing unit consists of a printing cylinder, an impression cylinder, an inking system, and a dryer. Ink is applied to the printing cylinder by an ink roll or spray, and the excess is removed by the doctor blade and returned to the ink fountain. The impression cylinder is covered with a resilient rubber composition that presses the paper into contact with the ink in the tiny cells of the printing surface. In multicolor printing, the printed ink is dried before the next impression so trapping wet inks is not a problem in gravure as it is in letterpress and lithography. Also, because of the fluid inks used, web tension does not cause any serious problems.

Gravure ink consists of pigment, a resin binder, and a volatile solvent. The ink is quite fluid and dries entirely by evaporation. For high-speed printing, the solvents are quite volatile, and the inking system must be enclosed. In most plants, when magazines and mail-order catalogs are printing with the same types of inks, the dryers between the printing units are connected to a solvent-recovery system to reduce problems with air pollution.

Table 1.2 Advantages and limitations of gravure printing

Advantages	Limitations
A simple process.	A direct transfer process.
Uses solvent-type inks.	High cost of cylinders with
Drying between printings.	chemical etching.
Continuous tone effect.	Need for proofing with full-size
Separation between image and	printing cylinders.
nonimage areas is mechanical.	Requires very smooth surfaces for
Less tension problems.	printing to prevent highlight skips.
No trapping problems.	
Prints varying amounts of ink	
resulting in brighter colors with	
cheaper pigments.	
Good color uniformity throughout run.	

Single-color conventional rotogravure yields excellent pictorial reproduction on a wide range of papers. Its reproduction of type matter and line drawings is inferior to the other processes because the screen reduces sharpness and readability. Color reproduction is mostly done in three and four colors on multicolor presses using cylinders with variable area–variable depth image elements. Gravure is widely used for newspaper magazine supplements, magazines, mail-order catalogs, cartons, labels, printing cellophane, plastic films, foils, floor coverings like linoleum and floor tiles, and plastic laminates. It is the most practical process for the printing of gold, bronze, aluminum, and opaque whites. For packaging and less demanding work, direct transfer or variable area cylinders are used.

A serious problem in gravure printing has been the necessity for very smooth papers to prevent "skips" in the printing. The introduction of trailing-blade-coated paper about 1957 was a big boon to gravure but it did not help in printing on newsprint or rough boards. The development of the electrostatic assist by the Gravure Research Institute has helped to solve the problem of skips and raise the general level of quality of gravure printing on all paper and paperboard stocks. See Table 1.2 for an overview of gravure printing advantages and limitations.

Lithographic printing

For nearly 100 years after Senefelder invented lithography in about 1800, all lithographic printing was done from hand-drawn or hand-transferred images on stone. The rotary principle which required conversion from stone to thin metal as the printing member was introduced about 1900 when images were transferred by hand from stones to metal plates using special transfer paper and inks.

Another revolutionary change occurred in 1906, when the offset principle was discovered for printing on paper and the offset press was introduced. Nearly all lithographic printing is done now by the offset principle and the term offset has become almost synonymous with lithography. Some relief (letterset) and even gravure (offset gravure) printing uses this principle particularly in packaging, but lithography uses it almost exclusively.

The offset principle provides a number of important advantages to lithography and, to some extent, to letterpress and gravure when it is used as follows:

1. The rubber printing surface conforms to the irregularities in the paper surface. Less printing pressure is needed. Print quality is improved, making possible halftones of good quality on rough-surfaced papers.

2. Paper does not contact the metal printing plate, reducing the possibility of abrasive wear and increasing the life of the plates.

3. Speed of printing is increased. Speeds over 10,000 impressions per hour are possible on sheet-fed presses, and over 30,000 per hour on web presses.

4. The image on an offset plate is "straight" reading instead of "reverse" reading, thus facilitating both preparation of the plates and correction of errors.

5. Less ink is required for equal coverage so drying time is reduced as well as the tendency for the ink to smudge or set off (from the front of one sheet to the back of the next sheet) in the delivery pile.

Sheet-fed presses are made in single color up to six colors in sizes from 17 × 22 in. (432 × 559 mm) sheet size to 55 × 78 in. (1397 × 1981 mm). Multicolor presses are made both in unit design and in common impression cylinder type in which two units consisting of inking, dampening, and plate and blanket cylinders share a common impression cylinder. A four- or six-color press of the latter design consists of combining two or three couples with one feeder and delivery. Some sheet-fed perfecting presses are used in book printing. Some are blanket-to-blanket, printing both sides of the sheet at the same time, and others turn the sheets over between impressions.

Most web offset presses are of the unit blanket-to-blanket type. These presses have been made with as many as twelve units feeding into two folders. A popular size for magazine printing is a perfecting blanket-to-blanket press which takes 38 in. (965 mm) wide rolls with cutoffs of 22.75 to 25.5 in. (578 to 648 mm), depending on the page sizes; this is referred to as a *16-page press*. When webs get much wider than 38 in. (965 mm) on blanket-to-blanket presses, serious problems with misregister on process color work called *fan-out* can be encountered. This is an effect of moisture and mechanical rollout, which causes the sheet to stretch sideways as it goes through the press, resulting in the first colors being printed emerging wider on the sheet than the succeeding colors. Wider width blanket-to-blanket presses up to 72 in. (1829 mm) are used for noncritical color printing. Common impression cylinder presses in widths up to 76 in. (1930 mm) are satisfactory for process color reproductions; the sheet is held firmly between impressions thus reducing the chance to stretch. On these presses, one side of the paper is printed at a time. Some web offset newspaper presses have combinations of blanket-to-blanket units for the single color pages and common impression units for color printing. A popular web offset press is the half-size or *8-page web.* There are also 32-page presses with maximum widths of 40 in.

Tension is a more serious problem on web offset presses than on letterpress web presses because tackier inks are used and more pull is needed on the paper to draw it through the press. The combination of the web tension, tacky inks, the dryer, and lightweight papers, especially in magazine printing, can cause serious problems with web breaks. New infeeds, including flying pasters with accumulators and special tension control devices consisting of inertia-compensated flywheels on dancer rollers have helped to reduce the incidence of web breaks on web offset presses. New dryers and paper rolls not more than a quarter of an inch out of round with tight edges also help reduce tension.

In the printing cycle on an offset lithographic press, water or fountain solution is transferred to the plate before it contacts the inking rollers. Very little moisture is required to accomplish proper dampening on a lithographic plate; the amount must be properly balanced to form a continuous film over the nonprinting areas as a barrier against the transfer of ink. The moisture adhering to the image areas is discontinuous so it does not interfere seriously with the transfer of ink. If too much fountain solution is used, its composition is incorrect, or its pH value is too low, moisture will transfer to the image areas and interfere with the proper transfer of ink in these areas. Thus, ink-water balance is a very critical factor in the optimum operation of lithographic presses. New dampening systems using direct feed and alcohol have been developed to minimize this problem but cannot eliminate it. Because of the critical ink-water balance, lithography produces more waste than either letterpress or gravure. It has many advantages to make up for this disadvantage, but on long runs, letterpress and gravure can be more cost effective. The successful use of driography, however, will retain the advantages of lithography without its disadvantages of having to maintain an ink-water balance and the additional waste it causes. Note Table 1.3, where the advantages and limitations of offset lithography are presented.

Screen printing

Much screen printing is done by hand with very simple equipment: table, screen frame, and squeegee. However, most commercial screen printing is

Table 1.3 Advantages and limitations of offset lithography

Advantages	Limitations
Low preparatory and plate costs.	Need for ink-water balance.
Uses the offset principle.	Need for tacky inks.
Uses a variety of presses.	Need for blanket.
Prints on rough surfaces.	Wet printing, causing trapping problems.
Both sheet-fed and web-fed presses can be used.	Overall contact of paper in impression nip.
	Need for purer papers.
	Moisture balance—color variation throughout run.
	Need stronger papers—thin ink films— poor gloss and gold.
	Paper piling—ink slur—dot doubling and spread.
	Poor register—fan-out, doubling, wrinkling.
	Waste at least twice that of letterpress and gravure.

done on power-operated presses, including roll-fed and sheet-fed presses, which run at speeds up to 300 ft/min, or over 4000 impressions per hour (IPH).

There are two types of power-operated presses. One type uses flat screens which require an intermittent motion as each screen is printed. Butts and overlaps require close register, which limits running speed. The latest type uses rotary screens with the squeegee mounted inside the cylinder and the ink pumped in automatically. These presses are continuous running, fast, and print continuous patterns with little difficulty.

The amount of ink applied in screen printing is far greater than in letterpress, lithography, or gravure, which accounts for some of the unusual effects produced by screen printing. Because of the heavy ink film, the sheets must be racked separately until dry, or passed through a heated tunnel or drier before they can be piled. UV inks are also used, and these can be cured with special UV curing equipment.

Screen printing can be completed on almost any material, and both line and halftone work can be printed. It is used for art prints, posters, decalomania transfers, greeting cards, menus, program covers, and wallpaper. Screen printing is important in the printing of textiles such as tablecloths, shower curtains, and draperies. It is particularly adaptable when printing on leather, metal, glass, wood, ceramic materials and plastics, both flat and finished molded forms. Screen printing is also used for short run heat transfer printing, in which inks with special subliming dyes are used for printing on paper. The paper prints are later transferred to textiles under heat and pressure.

Screen printing has distinct advantages for short runs because of the simplicity of the equipment needed. For longer runs, the advantage is soon lost since other printing methods are much faster and more economical. However, for most of the applications listed, screen printing is the only or most practical process.

Binding and finishing

After the printed sheet comes off the press, it must usually undergo other operations to become a finished product. Some printed sheets such as simple handbills, letterheads, announcements, posters, and calling cards—printed one up and with no bleed or trim—can be shipped without further processing. Some sheets are printed with more than one image up or a number of separate images, and these must be cut and trimmed before they can be delivered. Most printed sheets, however, become a part of something else, such as books or catalogs, and to accomplish the conversion, they are subjected to binding and finishing operations.

The operations of binding and finishing are as important a part of the converting operation as the printing. Binding and finishing cover a wide variety of operations. The work required to convert printed sheets or webs of paper into books, magazines, catalogs, folders, is called *binding*. The work required to make displays, labels, tags, folding boxes, greeting cards, and a variety of fancy packaging and advertising materials involves *finishing* operations.

Most printing is done on large sheets with a number of the same or different subjects on the sheets. Labels are varnished and cut to size after printing. Calendars are cut to size and stapled. In check printing, some are cut to size and stapled and some are perforated, cut, stapled, or drilled for insertion into binders. Greeting cards are embossed, die-cut, dusted with gold bronze, and folded. Some printed sheets are folded into pamphlets for mailing. Others are folded into signatures of 4 to 64 pages, which are later bound together in various ways to make books, magazines or catalogs. Letterheads and calling cards may be cut and wrapped in packages of 100 or reams. Most packaging printing is scored or creased, die-cut, stripped and glued for shaping into packages later.

The eight different types of binding are:
* *edition binding*: the binding of quantities of identical books, either case-bound, hardbound, or adhesive bound, usually called perfect binding;
* *job binding*, or extra binding: binding small quantities and special lots of books;
* *library binding*: special binding for private and public libraries;

- *pamphlet and trade binding*: binding leaflets, booklets, magazines, and some soft-covered books;
- *manifold or commercial binding*: binding multiple business forms such as purchase orders or sales books;
- *mechanical binding*: binding individual sheets of paper in a nonremovable form such as a plastic binder by a special binding device;
- *looseleaf binding*: binding individual sheets of paper in a removable form with special binders;
- *blankbook binding and ruling*: the manufacture of bound books with blank or ruled pages used for accounting, record keeping, receipts, or picture albums.

Finishing is a general term that includes the mounting, die-cutting, and easeling of displays; folding, collating, drilling, varnishing or laminating, embossing, bronzing, flocking, die-stamping, pebbling, beveling, deckling, gilt and marble edging of printed and unprinted materials; cutting, creasing, stripping and gluing of folding paper cartons; and the slotting and gluing of corrugated boxes. Some of the finishing operations are so closely allied to the printing that they are performed in-line with printing operations, especially on web-fed presses. In newspaper, magazine, and book printing, folded signatures are delivered from the press. In some types of packaging, especially on flexographic presses, the cutting, creasing, and stripping are done in-line with the printing.

Inks for letterpress and lithography

Printing inks consist of pigments or dyes dispersed in vehicles or binders; other ingredients such as solvents, driers, wetting agents, and waxes are added. The combination of pigments, dyes, vehicles, binders, and other ingredients used depends on the process and drying system employed. Most inks for sheet-fed letterpress and offset lithography consist of pigments dispersed in oleoresinous or drying oil vehicles modified with the addition of some drier and special compounds for adjusting inking conditions. Inks for web printing are heat-set, consisting of pigments dispersed in synthetic resins dissolved in high boiling petroleum solvents. Newsprint inks are dispersions of carbon black in mineral oil. Inks for flexography and gravure consist of pigments or dyes dispersed in natural or synthetic resins dissolved in water, alcohol, or other organic solvents.

Quick-set inks consist of dispersions of pigments in high molecular weight resins in a drying oil and a solvent. When printed on a sheet, the absorption of the solvent leaves the resin and oil almost dry on the surface, permitting sheet handling in a relatively short time after printing. *Super-quick set* inks demand a critical balance of resin and solvent and set about ten times faster than quick-set inks. These inks are used with new infrared drying devices.

In *high-gloss inks*, high molecular weight resins are used to wet pigments so the combination is not absorbed or drained into the sheet. *Metallic* inks consist of dispersions of aluminum and bronze in suitable synthetic resins. *Magnetic* inks consist of dispersions of a magnetic ferrosic oxide (Fe_3O_4) as the pigment in suitable varnishes. *Moisture-set* inks are dispersions of pigments in a resin soluble in a glycol, but insoluble in water. After printing, the image is passed under a stream of fine water spray or steam which separates or precipitates the resin pigment mixture.

The latest developments in printing inks are *radiation curing* inks, mostly *UV*, that do not involve solvents that can cause air pollution. UV curing inks are sensitized monomer or prepolymer systems that polymerize on exposure to high doses of UV radiation. *Electron beam* (EB) curing inks are used for coatings and other special uses. The hardware for EB curing is more expensive than UV, but energy consumption and ink costs are lower; more use of these inks may be made in the future.

All of these and other types of inks vary in body, length, tack, and drying characteristics, which are among the most important properties of inks besides color and color strength. These characteristics must be adjusted to the process and the paper used and are known as *rheological factors*.

Printed matter and inks must have other special characteristics besides the ones listed. Inks must dry so they are rub and smudge resistant. In labels and packaging, the printing must be scuff and scratch resistant. Printed subjects used for displays in windows and outdoors require inks that are light fast and resist fading. Heat-set and inks to be lacquered on a varnishing machine must be heat resistant so the pigments do not fade on exposure to heat. Ink used for soap wrappers must be alkali resistant and must not be changed by or bleed with the product. Labels or packaging to be lacquered or spirit varnished require inks that are alcohol or solvent proof to prevent bleeding in the solvents used in the lacquers. Liquor labels require alcohol proof inks. Hot-waxed wrappers must have inks that do not bleed in paraffin. The characteristics of inks and papers or other substrates used should be considered when selecting ink and materials.

Specialty printing

Printing can be highly specialized, such as printing for packaging, greeting cards, newspapers, magazines, books, business forms, and commercial printing. While the processes, techniques, and equipment for printing these specialties have already been described, they are considered here again to show how the various processes are used in specialty printing.

Packaging printing

Letterpress, once the predominant process for printing packages and labels, gradually has been replaced by lithography for the short and medium runs requiring good picture reproduction, and by gravure for the long runs. The 77- and 78-in. (1956- and 1981-mm) sheet-fed press has been popular in off-set lithography for printing packages and labels, but there is now a trend toward the use of 60-in. (1524-mm) presses and many of the new ones are designed so they can be equipped with UV curing systems with the UV lamps situated between printing stations and after printing.

Gravure printing for packaging is completed on narrow web-fed presses, up to about 48 in. (1219 mm); the rolls of printed matter are rewound for finishing at a later time on die-cutting or other finishing equipment. Direct transfer cylinders consisting of variable area images with essentially constant depth are used for printing illustrations. The tone scale is not as long as in lithography or in variable area–variable depth gravure, but the process is simpler.

Most of the flexographic printing done is for packaging. Almost all milk cartons are printed on stack-type presses and die-cutting and creasing are done in-line. Some unit-type presses are also used. Common impression cylinder presses are used for printing on extensible films and for fine-screen color process printing on paper. Bags are printed almost exclusively by the flexographic process. Most corrugated boxes are printed by the flexographic process on equipment known as printers and slotters. Some oil base inks are still being used on some corrugators to get the higher gloss, but the trend is toward the use of flexography with water base inks which set and dry almost instantly on the absorbent liner board. Most plates used for flexography are rubber, which is gradually being replaced by photopolymer plates for higher quality printing.

Greeting cards

A similar production pattern in greeting cards printing is followed by most greeting card publishers. The copy, art work, and most of the negatives or positives are prepared by the publisher and the printing is under contract by printers. With few exceptions, greeting card manufacturers do none of their own printing, but handle the often extensive finishing work.

Practically all greeting cards are printed by lithography and most of them are done in five color. The fifth color, usually a fluorescent pink, enhances fleshtones and reds. Holiday wrapping papers are printed by gravure and flexography.

Newspaper printing

Over 9,000 weekly newspapers and about 1,780 dailies are printed in the U.S. Some dailies print a Sunday edition. Newspapers were traditionally printed by letterpress, where the type was set by linecasting machines and was used to make stereotype plates. Because of the increasing labor costs of typesetting and engraving, most newspapers have taken advantage of economical phototypesetting and photomechanical platemaking methods.

The trend in the weekly and daily newspapers has been conversion to offset lithography. Almost 90% of the weeklies and over 80% of the daily newspapers are now printed by web offset. These represent most of the short and medium run newspapers and some large ones. Many of the long run daily newspapers are staying with letterpress and are considering other options such as photopolymer plates, DiLitho, and conversion of the presses to offset. DiLitho represents the conversion of letterpress newspaper presses to printing lithographic plates by the installation of special dampening systems in each printing station. Some are installing blanket cylinders to complete the conversion to offset. Others are installing satellite printing plants in suburban areas close to their distribution points; most of these plants are equipped with offset presses.

Table 1.4 shows the rate of conversion of daily newspapers to offset, and the proportion of total circulation they represented in the period from 1972 to 1980.

The table indicates that some of the larger newspapers are converting to offset. In the past several years, the *Detroit Free Press*, New York's *Newsday*, the *Chicago Tribune, The Washington Post,* the *New York Times,* and the *Los Angeles Times-Mirror* have converted. Not all conversions are to satellite plant operations.

American Newspaper Publishers Association (ANPA) Research Institute has developed a flexographic press for newspaper printing. If this is successful, it could have an effect on the trend to offset. The use of flexography could

Table 1.4   Conversion of daily newspapers to offset in the U.S., 1972–1980

	Daily Newspapers			Circulation (Millions)		
	Total	*Offset*	*% of Total*	*Total*	*Offset*	*% of Total*
1972	1749	868	49.6	62	11.6	18.8
1973	1761	976	55.4	62.6	15.9	25.4
1974	1774	1110	62.6	63.1	17.1	27.1
1975	1768	1173	66.3	61.9	17.2	27.8
1976	1779	1217	68.4	61.3	18.3	29.8
1977	1786	1260	70.5	61.6	19.4	31.5
1978	1781	1272	72.5	62.1	21.2	36.6
1979	1779	1340	75.3	62.2	26.2	42.8
1980	1767	1393	78.8	62.0	34.1	55.0

introduce the added advantage that water base inks can be used. This would eliminate any possibility of pollution from organic solvents and dependency on petroleum distillates.

A serious problem in considering the conversion of newspapers from letterpress to offset has been the accumulation of lint on the blankets of the offset press. Lint has been reduced considerably in the papermaking process by the use of two screens in place of the conventional single screen used on fourdrinier machines. The twin wire machines produce a sheet with essentially two wire sides so there is less loose lint or fines to collect on the blanket. Relief has also come in the development by chemical manufacturers of alkaline fountain etches which reduce the accumulation of lint on the blankets, and the introduction by several ink manufacturers of so-called "lint-free" inks, which are essentially ink-water emulsions.

Magazine publishing

Magazines traditionally have been printed in the United States by letterpress on machine coated paper with heat-set inks. In Europe, the majority of magazines are printed by gravure on supercalendered and some coated gravure paper. The main reason for the difference is believed to be the development in the U.S. of machine coated papers and heat-set inks before World War II, which encouraged the use of letterpress for magazine printing. Without these developments, European publishers were able to get better results from gravure. The gravure process developed to a greater extent in Europe, while letterpress prospered here. After World War II, there were many advancements in lithography with the introduction of better plates, web offset, machine coated papers, and heat-set inks for offset. This encouraged many publishers to try this process for shorter run magazines both here and abroad. Web offset has gradually replaced letterpress and is now the predominant process for magazine printing. In Europe, gravure is giving way to web offset.

The other division in magazine publishing is between general interest and special interest magazines. The market for the general interest magazine has been eroded by competition from other sources of entertainment and other media such as television and radio, which has resulted in reduced readership and advertising revenues. *Saturday Evening Post* was the first to go, *Look* stopped publication in 1971, and *Life* in 1972. Other general interest magazines changed format size and reduced circulation.

In the past ten years, more than five times as many new magazines have been published as have failed. Most of the new magazines are special interest publications, which are increasing in number, size, and circulation. More than half of these are printed by web offset and the list grows steadily.

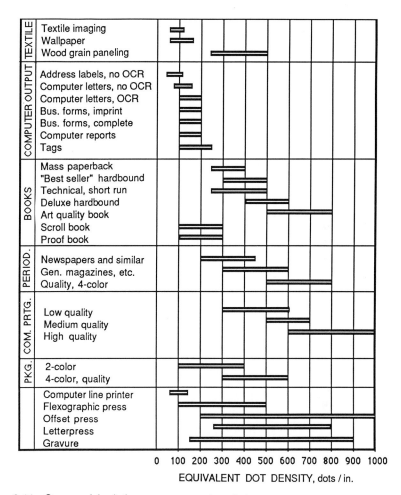

Fig. 2.11 Commercial printing processes and markets.

All the printing methods, both the nonimpact and conventional, have one thing in common: the paper moves to, over, through, or under the printing unit. It is the paper, the substrate, that must be moved in relation to the printing unit itself. What is the fastest process that handles paper available today? It is a modern winder as used to finish rolls of paper for shipment. Both of the winders illustrated in Fig. 2.12 are widely used in the industry. But the MIR winder and similar ones known as *center wind* winders are definitely more modern and do produce mechanically better rolls at top speeds. Both these winders are running in many paper mills in the world today in excess of 6,000 ft/min and up to 300 in. in width, or wider. They

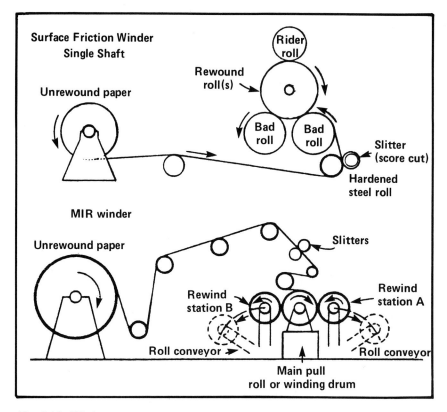

Fig. 2.12 Winders.

can only produce rolls. Taking paper away from this machinery either in sheets or in folded signatures cannot be done. Rolls only may be shipped due to the very high speed. Both these systems are extremely flexible insofar as basis weight or caliper is concerned. In addition to running in excess of 6000 ft/min and 300 in. wide, these winders will also run basis weights ranging from as low as 25 lb 25 x 38 – 500, a lightweight form bond type sheet, up to 28-pt coated bottle carrier board, which is extremely stiff and heavy. A maximum of 6 ft and probably an average of 4 ft from position to position is the open length of paper in any one point in a winder system. If a printing system is devised which will print on each side of the paper in this open distance, a printing process can operate in excess of 6000 ft/min and up to the full width of 300 in. or more. This might be considered as the limiting factor in the speed of any printing process: actual, experimental, or theoretical. Table 2.3 contains a summary of impactless variable printing methods.

Table 2.3 Summary of impactless variable printing methods

	Thermal	*Magnetic*	*Electro-graphic*	*Electropho-tographic*	*Ink jet*
Procedure	Heat develops colored image	Develops toner image on magnetic tape–transferred to paper and fused	Charge transfer by stylus to dielectric side of paper	Light developed image is toned, transferred to paper, fused	Ink droplets transferred from jets to paper
Paper	Special	Plain	Special insulated coated paper	Plain	Plain
Area of Use	Teletype output and related	Teletype output and related	Computer output, alphanumeric, plotting, graphics	Computer output	Teletype, computer output, specialized imaging
Extent of Application	Thousands in use	Hundreds in use	Thousands in use	Thousands in use	Hundreds in use
Maximum Speed in Characters Per Second	120	400	40,000	28,000	125,000

Summary

The changing nature of originating sources is causing basic changes in the growth rates of some established nonimpact printing, duplicating, and copying methods. This new communications environment, however, has created steep growth patterns for printing systems that can fit in the computer-electronics communications systems of the future.

The best opportunities using ZnO coating technology are in the liquid and dry toner electrophotographic offset plate market which appears to be growing at the rate of 15–25% per year.

Dielectric copy systems designed to meet the printing requirements of nonimpact computer systems have excellent growth potential.

Variable and fixed information printing using dielectric technology will have a deep impact on utility printing and on the forms market.

The use of thermal and electrosensitive imaging systems will increase rapidly as they fit the specific needs for nonimpact printing tied to electronic calculators, micro- and mini-computers, point of sale cash registers, and various banking systems.

Ink-jet printing has great potential for high-speed, computer-oriented variable printing. Section XI, Future Trends, contains more information on nonimpact dot matrix printing of digitalized information, including references for further study.

Section III
Groundwood
Paper Grades

J. R. Gunning, Editor

3
Groundwood Paper Grades

J. R. Gunning

Introduction

In many parts of the world groundwood grades are called mechanical printings. Both names indicate a difference in composition from free sheets, which are made of chemical fiber. The manufacture of groundwood is a mechanical process, and the pulp has very specific properties. The fibers are wood with all the natural chemicals in the tree such as lignin, hemicellulose, and sugars still present. They are obtained by pressing round wood against a gritty grindstone that tears them out; the fibers are continuously flushed away with water. Unfortunately the pulp that results does not make a strong enough sheet for papermaking or printing. Reinforcing with kraft or sulfite pulp is needed.

There are many grades of paper that contain mechanical fiber, and newsprint is by far the most common. Roto news is a modified sheet for a special printing process and end use. Special sheets which contain high proportions of mechanical fiber and are often made in other basis weights are directory and catalog. Many business papers suitable for typing and computer printouts are now made with a proportion of this less expensive fiber.

During the last decade a great deal of research has been done with refiners to make mechanical pulp. The work has been very successful and new processes are replacing the grinder method. Many acronyms are now used to differentiate the refiner processes: refiner groundwood (RG); thermomechanical pulp (TMP); thermochemical mechanical pulp (TCMP), etc.

One of the original objectives of the new technology was to make a mechanical fiber that would form a sheet of paper without the addition of chemical pulp. This has been done, but has not yet replaced the conventional system in many mills. The refiner process accepts chips and sawdust while grinders require round wood. The process lends itself to integration with the lumber business and the utilization of more of the tree, which is most attractive when fiber is becoming scarce.

On the other hand, more energy is required at present. It has been found that the stone grinding process can be made to yield an improved product when done in a pressure vessel and the energy demands are lower than for refining.

The objective of eliminating chemical pulp is a result of the stringent anti-pollution laws now in effect. The effluent from chemical pulping is not only objectionable, but contains much of the wood which is salable. Simple economics dictate that as much of the tree (the raw material) should go into the product (paper) as possible, with the minimum of energy expended.

Newsprint

History

The history of newspapers is linked to the history of paper, ink, and printing presses. Considerable time, manpower, and expense could be expended on books that were going to be kept and treasured, but inexpensive materials were needed for the printing of current news.

The development did not occur quickly, but finally resulted in a distinct technology. Charles Fenerty of Nova Scotia suggested the use of ground-wood in 1839, while Buntin of Valleyfield, Quebec reported his similar efforts to make an inexpensive paper in 1866. During the same period, Keller and Voelter of Germany worked on groundwood papers between 1844 and 1870. According to the records in the Cleveland Public Library, this type of paper was generally accepted for newspapers by 1844.

Groundwood fiber was not only inexpensive but had very desirable properties. It made paper opaque and very absorbent; this enabled the inkmaker to make a very inexpensive special ink for the printer. News ink is made of about 12% carbon black or soot and a residual petroleum oil. It does not dry by oxidation, polymerization, or evaporation, but simply soaks into the paper. This happens quite quickly so there is no need for drying ovens or time. Also, it is generally known that oil on paper makes it transparent. The high opacity of groundwood can mask this transparency to a great extent. Another good property of groundwood is its bulkiness. Lead stereos were developed as a quick way to make printing plates. They were not perfectly uniform but the cushion provided by the paper resulted in a very acceptable job.

According to Straus, stereotypes were invented in the latter half of the eighteenth century, which was well before groundwood was accepted (1). From that time until the 1960s there was little change in the general procedure for printing a newspaper. The written copy was given to a Linotype operator who worked a keyboard like a typewriter and the machine produced the letters in cast lead. These slugs were set up on a flat piece of steel the size of a newspaper page, approximately 15 × 22 in. A flong or mat was made of this type by pressing a thick piece of impregnated paper board onto it. The mat was hardened with heat so a mold was formed; the lead stereos that were put on the press were cast from the mold.

By the middle of the twentieth century, a revolution began. Computers were becoming efficient and inexpensive; newspapers started to assemble type matter via computers. The result was a sheet of paper or a piece of film. The process was termed "cold composition" to differentiate it from cast molten lead, or "hot composition."

Other methods of making a printing plate had to be found. By the early 1960s some publishers had decided to scrap their old stereo letterpress machines and buy new offset presses. However, this was not practical for many publishers whose presses were relatively new, and the millions of dollars spent on a new press could not be justified. However, those who did switch to web offset printing demanded certain properties in the standard newsprint grade to fit their particular requirements. The publishers who could not switch away from letterpress printing had to find another way of making plates. Many suppliers to the newspaper industry worked on the problem and plates made by the photographic method were developed. Initially, the proposed systems were adaptations of the existing technology of photoengraving. For instance, zinc or magnesium could be etched to leave raised parts for letterpress printing. The metal sheets were thin so they would not replace stereos without a backing. Another approach was to etch a metal master and then make a mold or flong to cast stereos. The chemical industry developed a number of plastic plates. The term "shallow relief" was coined to describe this form of letterpress printing. In the early 1970s most brands of plates on the market were all metal. Most plastic plates now are metal-backed plastic. Modifications to the plastic polymers are being made constantly by the suppliers.

Direct lithography for printing on newsprint was first attempted in Scandinavia, but in June 1970 the Research Institute of the American Newspaper Publishers Association (ANPA/RI) published a report (Bulletin 1018) on investigating converting stereo presses to use direct lithography. This system puts the image directly on the paper from the metal plate, while in offset, the image is transferred first to a rubber surface and then to the paper. ANPA/RI worked with American equipment suppliers to make it a commercial process and patented the name DiLitho. It appears to be the most demanding system on paper and presently seems to be losing rather than gaining popularity.

From the foregoing it is obvious that the demands on newsprint have undergone a drastic change. For a century letterpress printing with lead stereos and a simple ink put only moderate demands on the paper. The American

Newspaper Publishers Association now lists the printing methods as stereo, letterpress (shallow-relief/plastic plates), offset, and DiLitho. Each of these methods has its own demands on the paper both from a runnability as well as a printability point of view. The methods become even more important when new types of fiber are used in the paper furnish.

Economics

Newsprint is purchased by publishers as a substrate for their printing of the written word. The number and volume of newspapers in a country is an indication of its society. A large number of newspapers indicates good communication in a country, not only of news and social conditions, but also of commerce. Advertising accounts form a very large part of the makeup of newspapers in the Western world and they finance the cost of publishing to a great extent. Undeveloped countries do not use and cannot afford as much paper per capita as Western Europe and North America. The increase in paper consumption is a good indication of an improving economy (Fig. 3.1).

Newsprint was probably one of the first "disposables." It is the substrate which carries a printed message to the public and, once read, is discarded. It must have only sufficient durability for this task before it is thrown out. For this reason, the least expensive paper is desirable.

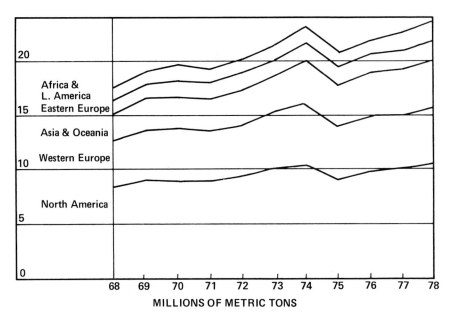

Fig. 3.1 Worldwide demand for newsprint — 1978 (courtesy of Canadian Pulp and Paper Association).

Printing requirements

Newspaper publishers and printers have two general requirements of newsprint regardless of the kind of press or the printing process used: *runnability and printability*. Nearly every property of the paper affects one or the other.

Newspapers operate on a very tight and inflexible schedule. The deadline for news and advertising is set for the last possible moment. The pages have to be planned and prepared by pasting up all the strips of type from the photocomposing machines as well as veloxes of news photos and advertisements. The pasteups are photographed and printing plates are made from the negatives. The plates are then put on the press and the press is webbed up with newsprint. The press produces newspapers at a known rate so definite numbers of them reach the mail room for distribution at a calculated time. Trucks, trains, and aircraft leave on schedule to have the product in the reader's hands within minutes of the normal time, e.g. to read on the 7:15 a.m. train. The most critical link in the chain of events is the behavior of the paper on the press. Web breaks are press stoppers on a press the same way they are on a paper machine. Communication between a pressroom and the paper mill is expressed in "breaks per 100 rolls" or its reciprocal "rolls per break." Less than 5 breaks/100 rolls from all causes is normally expected.

Newspaper press configurations

General

While there are many more small pressrooms than large ones, it is the large metropolitan papers that account for the major part of the paper tonnage. They have a number of presses; for this reason, a typical press in a large daily will be discussed.

Both letterpress and offset presses are built to run at about 60,000 newspapers per hour, *straight run*, which is stated as 60,000 impressions per hour (IPH). A *collect run* describes the process where the two plates around the cylinder are different so only half as many newspapers are printed. The average size of papers for cities in the U.S. is 64 pages for the morning daily paper, 56 for the afternoon/evening papers and 196 pages for the Sunday edition. Some simple arithmetic may help to give a better understanding of the setup. A standard broad sheet page is approximately 22 in. long and 15 in. wide.

Width of press = 4 pages = 4 × 15 in. = 60 in.
Circumference of cylinder = 2 pages = 2 × 22 in. = 44 in.

Number of pages per revolution of a printing unit (two couples) collect, printed both sides of the paper = 2 × 2 × 4 = 16 pages.

(sides) × (pages around) × (pages across)

For example, if a paper has 128 pages and is printed collect, the number of 60-in. white rolls needed on the press at one time is:

$$\frac{128}{16} = 8 \text{ rolls.}$$

There are eight full rolls of newsprint, one for each printing unit, at a time. Since these webs are twice as wide as the double broad sheet page, all the webs are slit. The actual number of slitters running depends on the way the press is webbed. The 16 printed webs that reach the delivery station or folder, as it is called, must be stacked together and folded in half before being cut off in 22-in. lengths. The cut off packs are folded a second time before they are sent to the mail room. An example:

Area of paper in 128 pages printed both sides.

$$= \frac{128}{2} \times 22 \times 15 = 21120 \text{ in.}^2$$
$$= 147 \text{ ft}^2$$

Standard newsprint weighs 30 lb per 3000 ft^2

$$\text{Weight of a newspaper} = \frac{147}{3000} \times 30 = 1.47 \text{ lb}$$

Production per hour collect — 30,000 newspapers
— 44,100 lb
— 20 metric tons

$$\text{Speed of each web} - \frac{60,000}{2} \text{ rph} \times \frac{44}{12} \times \frac{1}{60} = 1833 \text{ fpm}$$

The arithmetic example requires some explanation. The printing press can be set with duplicate printing plates around the plate cylinder so that every print in that machine direction strip (15 in.) is the same, i.e., a straight run. If the plates are different and the pages alternate, arrangements have to be made at the folder. It is called a collect run. While the tonnage of paper through the press is the same, only one-half the rated count is obtained with a collect run. If the 128-page example had been run straight, 16 rolls of paper would have been needed but production would have been 60,000 IPH instead of 30,000 IPH.

Fig. 3.2 depicts a Goss Headliner press. In some respects, it is similar to a paper machine. The operating floor is the second level. In the basement,

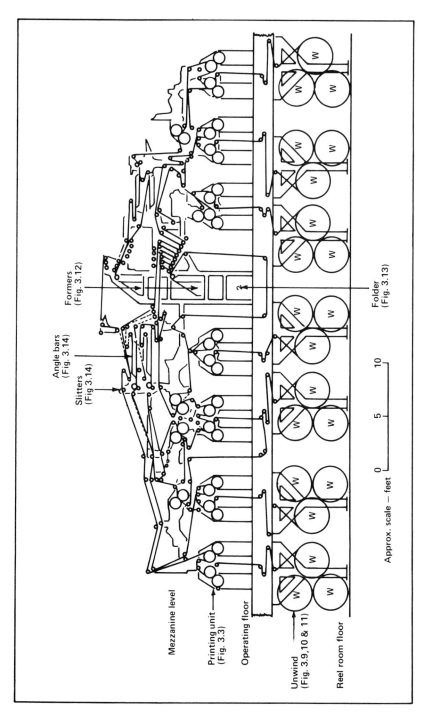

Fig. 3.2 Schematic of a Goss Metropolitan press (courtesy of Rockwell International).

which is called the reel room, the white rolls from the paper mills are put up on unwind stands (W in the figure). The paper from one roll on each unwind is threaded up through openings in the ceiling to the printing units on the main floor. After the webs are printed on both sides, they go up to a third level where they are slit and perhaps moved sideways with angle bars, and taken over to the folder which is in the middle of the press.

On the third level, or mezzanine, special printing units for color or other additions to the printing are located. The entire machine is about four stories high or about 30 ft tall depending on the particular installation. The length of the press depends on the number of printing units. In the example of eight units and one folder, the length is approximately 60 ft. Large press rooms often arrange as many as 24 units with 4 or 5 folders in line to provide flexibility. Some web leads get to be extremely long.

The illustration indicates the complexity of the web leads from the printing units to the folder. The printed pages must be *in register* when they come together at the folder so that each web is run over adjustable take-up rollers to compensate for the length of the web. The system of collecting the webs can be seen to the right of the formers in the figure. It is not uncommon for there to be 500 to 700 ft of paper between the reels and the folder, much of it full width but much of it slit. Each web starts with two edges. When the webs are slit, more edges are formed. Since most breaks start at an edge, the possibility of a web break is great.

Printing couples

The principles of printing have already been discussed in this book, but a few words about newspaper printing may help at this time. The methods currently used are stereo, direct letterpress, DiLitho, and offset lithography. The first three methods are done on the conventional printing presses developed for lead stereos. Figs. 3.3 and 3.4 show a schematic of a printing unit and the manner in which the paper web is threaded through it. The raised lead type is mounted on the plate cylinders (rolls 10 and 13 in Fig. 3.3). The impression cylinders which press the paper against the type are covered with a resilient material (rolls 11 and 12). Each pair prints one side of the sheet so that two pairs, couples, are needed for both sides.

When shallow-relief or plastic plates are used because cold composition has been adopted, the diameter of the cylinders must be built up with saddles (Fig. 3.5). DiLitho plates are also thin so that similar saddles are needed.

Fig. 3.6 shows an enlarged view of the surface of the plate cylinder dressed with a stereo or a thin plate. The steel is built to take a printing plate 0.440 in. thick. The lead stereos are machined to this thickness. Thin plates are only about 0.030 in. so the difference is made up by a saddle made of aluminum or magnesium. The pressman has to handle 41 lb when a stereo

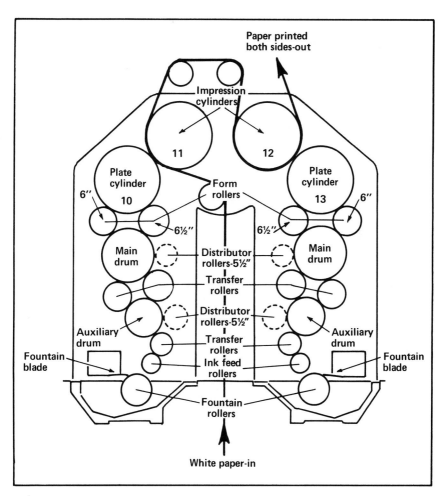

Fig. 3.3 Schematic of Goss letterpress printing unit (courtesy of Rockwell International).

is put on but only 0.4 lb with a thin plate. The saddles are left on permanently.

A number of companies have developed systems to adapt letterpress presses to offset lithography. Most publishers who decide to change to offset buy new presses. Fig. 3.7 shows the arrangements and webbing of one unit of an offset press. The web passes straight through between the rubber blanket-covered impression cylinders.

Offset means the image from the planographic plate is printed onto a rubber covered roll which transfers it to the paper. Since the flat rubber surface contacts the paper, the impression roller which backs up the paper can also

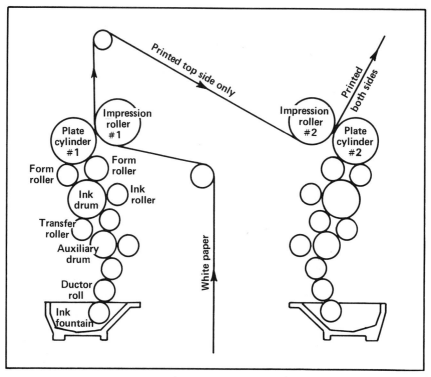

Fig. 3.4 Schematic of letterpress printing couple (courtesy of Rockwell International).

be used to print, thus both sides of the web can be printed at once. The operation is referred to as *perfecting*. The web lead is made more simple in the printing unit but all other parts of the operation are the same as for letterpress.

When two rollers are in contact they form a *nip*, and a nip pressure results. The pressure may be controlled in a number of ways. In a calender stack, the weight of the rolls creates nip pressure. Loading on the journals with weights or hydraulic cylinders also creates nip pressure. If the journal bearings are locked solidly, nip pressure on a web depends on the elasticity of the roll surface and the material of the web. Fig. 3.8 illustrates the nip arrangement for a pair of impression rolls on an offset press. At the ends of the rolls are solid metal rings referred to as bearers. The bearings are loaded so that the blankets are compressed and the rolls run bearer-to-bearer. The amount of compression or the pressure on the paper is given in thousandths of an inch. The illustration shows that the surface of the blanket is 0.003 in. above bearer on each roll. The paper is about 0.003 in. thick so that the impression is given as "9 thous." In Fig. 3.5, a similar situation is shown for letterpress printing. In that case, the hard type is bearer height and the over packing is all on the impression cylinder. Some presses do not have bearers so the pitch line of the gears is used as the reference.

The current popularity of the various printing methods for newspapers is shown in Tables 3.1, 3.2, 3.3, and 3.4.

Other components of a newspaper press

Reel Room. While some smaller newspaper presses and many commercial presses are arranged with the unwind stands for new paper on the main operating floor, the larger newspaper presses are supplied from the reel room under the press. Fig. 3.2 shows three rolls for each printing unit. The arrangement is to allow flying pasters so the press need not be stopped when rolls of paper are used up and new ones are needed. Fig. 3.9 illustrates the unwind system or *reel* for a typical press.

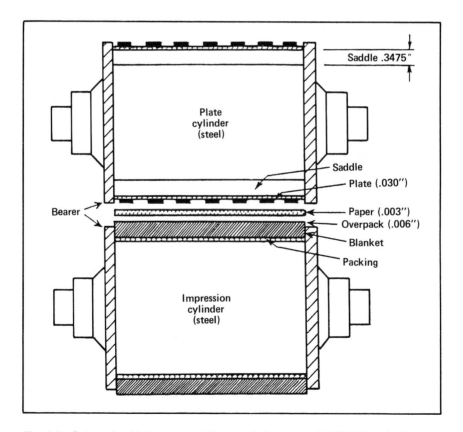

Fig. 3.5 Schematic of letterpress printing couple (courtesy of Abitibi-Price, Inc.).

The reel has a central shaft on which three-armed chucking and paster spiders for supporting the paper rolls are rigidly mounted. Rolls of newsprint are supported between the spiders by ball-bearing mounted spindles extending into the core of the rolls from the end of each spider arm. The rolls are indexed smoothly into position for loading, makeup, and infeeding into the unit by the revolving drive. The drive motor is furnished with a magnetic brake so that the reel may be stopped instantly in any desired position. The reel is indexed to any desired position when the operator presses the forward or reverse push buttons. The core of an expired roll is easily removed and a new roll loaded on the reel either during the run or when the press is stopped.

A push button-controlled hydraulic margin system permits the reel to be moved horizontally in either direction for sidelay positioning. A cocking roller, pivoted on one end and controlled by a handwheel, compensates for webs coming from unevenly wound rolls.

The tension system consists of tension belts, sensing roller (governor roller), air cylinders, tension control panel, and associate controls (Fig. 3.10). This

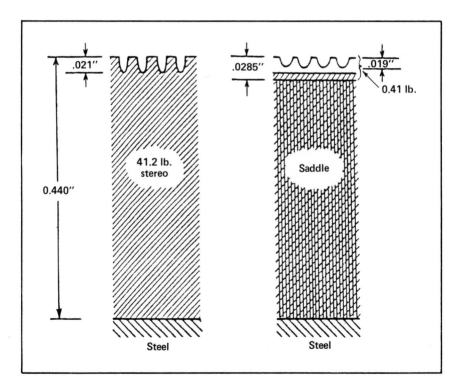

Fig. 3.6 Comparison of stereo to saddle and thin plate (courtesy of Abitibi-Price, Inc.).

system provides for running web tension variations and emergency stops. Web tension is maintained constant to allow paper to be fed continuously without breaking.

Web tension is regulated by air cylinders connected to the tension belts which press against the running roll of paper. The belts brake the roll in proportion to the force exerted by the air cylinders. The web from the roll travels around the sensing roller suspended from the steel pivot shaft. The force exerted on the sensing roller by the web causes the roller to swing around the pivot shaft axis. Web tension measurements from the sensing roller are conveyed to the tension control panel regulating the pressure on the air cylinders. The air cylinders in turn govern the pressure of the tension belts on the running roll.

The pasting sequence in Fig. 3.11 shows the expiring roll at the 4 o'clock position and the new roll at the 12 o'clock position. The next roll to be used is in the 8 o'clock position where it is prepared for the paster. Preparation includes cutting the end of the paper to form a series of v's which are then painted with a very tacky glue and kept from unwinding with perforated

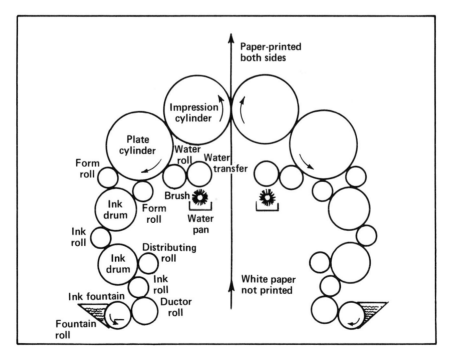

Fig. 3.7 Schematic of perfecting offset press showing ink and water systems, and plate and impression cylinders (courtesy of Rockwell International).

stickers. The glue is in line with the slot in the core in which the stub shaft key fits.

When a full roll is running, it is in the 2 or 3 o'clock position. As it expires, the spider is rotated to move it down to 4 o'clock. This brings the incoming roll to the 12 o'clock position where a set of belts start it spinning at the speed of the press. There is a timing system connected to the key in the chuck and thus to the pasted end. When the operator judges the butt is small enough, he presses a button which causes a brush to press the presently running web against the incoming roll. The timer controls the exact moment so that the glued end meets the web; the new paper pastes to the old, the perforated tabs break, and the new paper is on its way. There is a double web momentarily, then a knife cuts off the old web. The spider is then rotated to put the empty core in position 8 o'clock for removal and a new roll put on.

Formers. The last operations before the newspapers go to the mailroom are forming, folding, and cutting. The former is where the printed webs are

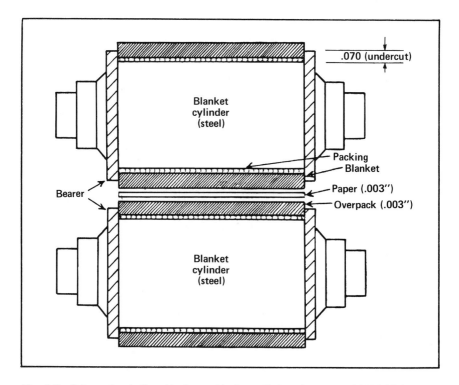

Fig. 3.8 Schematic of offset blanket to blanket cylinders (courtesy of Abitibi-Price, Inc.).

brought together, one on top of another and folded. The bottom sheet is against the steel plate and must slide. The other webs must stay flat and not cockle or wrinkle. Newsprint that is not pliable enough or is too dry sometimes bunches on the nose of the former, which causes a series of small creases ending in splits. The inside sheet or the outside sheet will often split on the fold. Fig. 3.12 shows four formers; the top two are called *balloon formers*. They are flat, triangular plates set on an angle with the nose down; the edges are rounded. The 30-in. wide webs are drawn over and folded down the center and creased with a set of rollers. The number of plys varies but is usually six. When all four formers are used, the newspaper has four sections.

Folders. The folded webs are threaded into a folder, a very noisy and complicated piece of equipment. It cuts the folded webs the correct length, puts the second fold across the page, and tucks the sections together. When collect runs are being made, it stores every second print so that the paper is properly collated (Fig. 3.13).

Large newspapers are quite thick and bulky, so when they are folded, the outside sheets are quite strained. Splitting often occurs if the paper is too dry or does not have sufficient elasticity or flexibility.

Table 3.1 U.S. daily newspapers—1979 (ANPA Special Reports 80-5, 80-6.)

Printing process	Number of newspapers	Percent of newspapers	Circulation (millions)	Percent of circulation
Offset	1340	75.3	26.8	42.8
Direct Letterpress	336	18.9		
DiLitho	82	4.6	35.8	57.2
Stereotype	21	1.2		
Total	1779	100.0	62.6	100.0

Table 3.2 Canadian daily newspapers—1979

Printing process	Number of newspapers	Percent of newspapers	Circulation (millions)	Percent of circulation
Offset	83	69.2	1.9	39.3
Direct Letterpress	31	25.8		
DiLitho	4	3.3	3.0	60.7
Stereotype	2	1.7		
Total	120	100.0	4.9	100.0

Angle bars and bay window. Paper mills ship full rolls (approx. 60 in.), three-quarter rolls (approx. 45 in.), half rolls (approx. 30 in.) and dinkies (approx. 15 in.) to the pressrooms. The make up of a newspaper can vary a lot depending on the number of pages needed for an edition. The 58 or 60 in. full rolls and three quarter rolls must be slit on the press at all times but half rolls must also be slit sometimes. In many cases a web may be printed on the back side of a press but must be moved laterally to go to a former on the front. Fig. 3.14 illustrates a web (60 in.) being slit and the front half being shifted sideways for placement on top of the back half.

For certain pages printed in color or for editorial reasons, a printing press configuration sometimes requires a web to be turned upside down. A set of bars called a *bay window* turns the web over (Fig. 3.15).

Paper considerations for runnability

Transit damage

The first time a customer sees the paper from a mill is when it is unloaded from the truck or box car. If the wrappers are torn or scuffed, they have

Table 3.3 U.S. newspapers (ANPA Special Report 80-6)

Newspapers	Number	Percent
Letterpress	439	24.7
Total	1779	100.0

Printing plate system	Number	Percent of shallow relief	Percent of total
Napp	166	49.4	37.8
Letterflex (Grace)	83	24.7	18.9
Merrigraph (Hercules)	50	14.9	11.4
Dyna-Flex	27	8.0	6.1
Magnesium	5	1.5	1.1
Dycril	2	0.6	0.5
Flatbed	2	0.6	0.5
Injection Moulding	1	0.3	0.2
	336	100.0	76.5
DiLitho	82		18.7
Stereotype	21		4.8
	439		100.0

a bad appearance which creates doubts in the customer's mind. If the headers are torn off or damaged, the roll ends may be damaged. A small nick in the edge of the web can trigger a break. If the cores are crushed, the chucks on the spiders (Fig. 3.9) will not go in so the roll cannot be used. Care in roll winding, wrapping, and loading helps the roll to travel well.

Flat rolls or *starred* rolls are often blamed on the carrier. In some cases this is true, but very frequently it is the fault of poor winding. The paper must be tight on the core and the tension in the web should decrease as the outside is approached (*2*). A roll of paper is a laminated cylindrical structure of plies of paper laid down under tension. Measurements with strain gauges and pressure transducers have shown that the compressive forces of the outer plies of the cylinder cancel the tension of those underneath so that most of the paper winds up under compression. Only a very few wraps on the outside remain in tension. The neutral axis of a roll should be within a fraction of an inch of the outside. Soft winding near the center with tight winding on top will cause a roll to telescope or star under shock. Rolls that are too hard are very susceptible to bursting and puncturing. Nails in the floor of a rail car or truck can damage a roll badly; even very small irregularities are harmful because of the continuous vibration of the vehicle and the jarring of the road bed.

Table 3.4 Canadian newspapers (ANPA Special Report 80-6)

Newspapers	Number	Percent
Letterpress	37	30.8
Total	120	100.0

Printing plate system	Number	Percent of shallow relief	Percent of total
Napp	19	61.2	51.4
Merrigraph (Hercules)	7	22.6	18.9
Letterflex (Grace)	2	6.5	5.4
Nyloprint	2	6.5	5.4
Magnesium	1	3.2	2.7
	31	100.0	83.8
DiLitho	4		10.8
Stereotype	2		5.4
	37		100.0

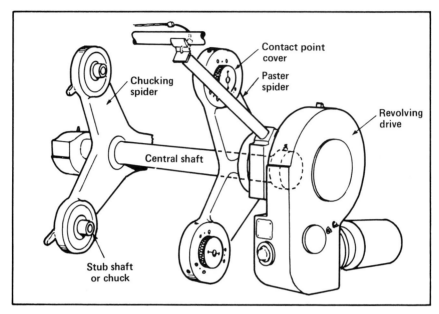

Fig. 3.9 Goss reel (courtesy of Abitibi-Price, Inc.).

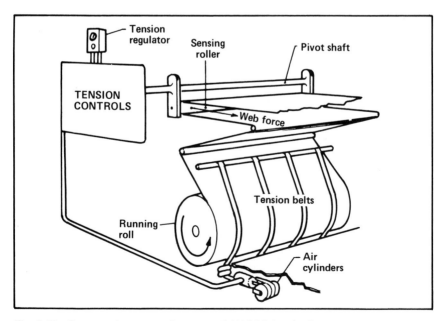

Fig. 3.10 Goss tension system (courtesy of Abitibi-Price, Inc.)

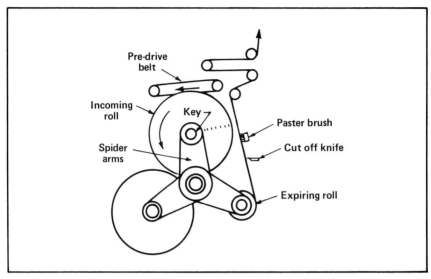

Fig. 3.11 Schematic of a reel (courtesy of Abitibi-Price, Inc.).

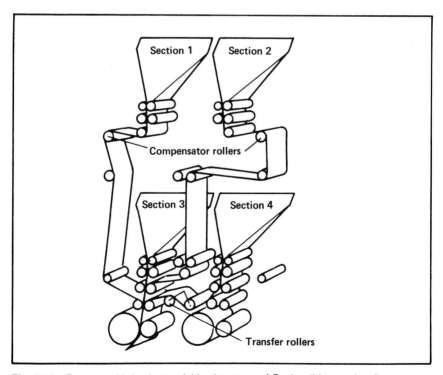

Fig. 3.12 Formers with leads to a folder (courtesy of Rockwell International).

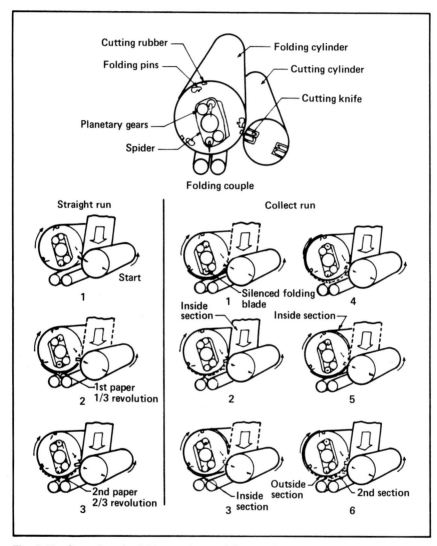

Fig. 3.13 Operation of a folder running straight or collect (courtesy of Rockwell International).

Splices are important in any paper used in a web press. They must be made properly when the rolls are wound since they must run through all the press stations, including slitting, and not let go. Surplus paper, particularly ahead of the splice, must be avoided since it has a great tendency to snag and cause a web break. Press stoppers are caused by poor splices, regardless of the printing method or folders used.

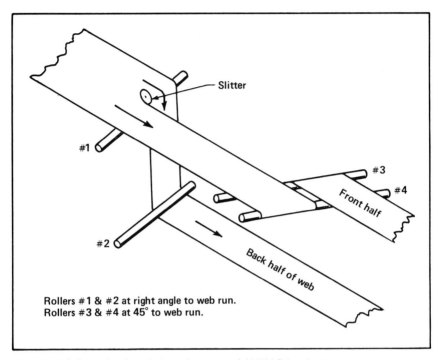

Fig. 3.14 Schematic of angle bars (courtesy of Abitibi-Price, Inc.).

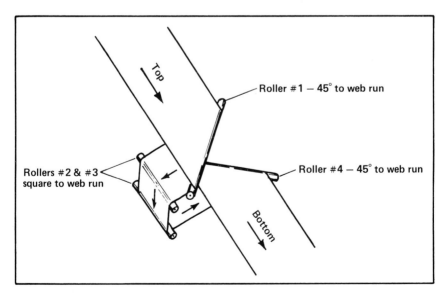

Fig. 3.15 Schematic of bay window (courtesy of Abitibi-Price, Inc.)

Press unwind

At this station, the white rolls are put in the spider by swinging them between chucks. The cores and metal tips must fit well so that the rolls will turn smoothly. If the rolls are out of round, the unwinding web will jerk and give uneven tensions even though there are dancer rolls to compensate. A *missed paster* is caused by improper preparation by the crew, a malfunction of the automatic equipment, or a shift of the core in the roll, poorly wound white rolls, and paper with slack edges or bagginess.

Slipping cores is a common term thought to mean the paper slips forward around the core. However, research has shown that when a roll is rotated, as it is with the speed belt, the core rotates faster than the paper (*3,4*). It is an internal gear effect and will move the slot out of line with the glue on the leading edge of the paper. The automatic system which is timed by the key in the slot will cause the brush to press the outgoing web at the wrong time. It is a fault at the mill caused by the winder or crew.

The white roll is carefully inspected when it is put on the press. It is not recommended that the body wrap be taken off until the roll is swung between the chucks so that the paper is protected until the last few minutes. While this means there is protection against mechanical damage, it also means pro-

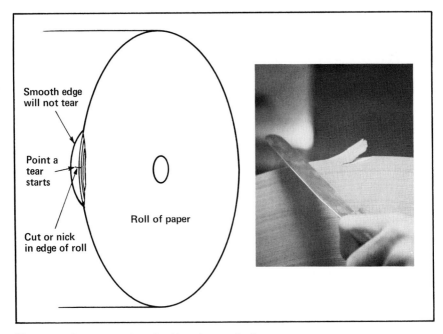

Fig. 3.16 Sciving a white roll with a damaged edge.

tection against moisture. If the humidity is as high as it should be, moisture welts will quickly form, and this can cause creasing.

If the edges of the roll show bruises or nicks, they are scived with a sharp knife. This means a smooth, cresent-shaped piece is taken out which will remove the nick and prevent a tear extending across the web when under tension (Fig. 3.16). Force is concentrated at the end of a crack, but a smooth edge will distribute the force. The knife is held at about 45 degrees to the horizontal so that a number of plies of paper are cut. The arc cut in the top ply must be large enough to include the end of the crack. In each succeeding layer of paper, the segment becomes smaller. There is a practical limit to the size of the top segment since it will show as a piece out of the edge of the newspaper page, although many publishers will accept the condition since so much paper can be saved. During the threading of a press, webs with cracks several inches long are coaxed through by hand tearing the segments out that contain the cracks or edge tears.

As little paper as possible is slabbed off a new roll since there is no repulper or beater in a press room to reuse the paper. The loss is easy to calculate. Each sheet of paper taken off a 40 in. (1016 mm) diameter roll, assuming 60 in. (1524 mm) wide, weighs 237 g, while a sheet from a butt 6 in. in diameter (152 mm) weighs 35.6 g. The ratio is 6.66:1. A quarter-inch slab off the outside is about the same amount of paper as 1.5 in. at the butt, which would be 43 lb (19.7 kg) or 2.7% of the total paper in a roll.

The printing units

The web run through the letterpress printing units is more complicated than through offset units due to the manner in which the paper is nipped between the printing surface and the impression roll. In letterpress, the type is forced into the surface while in offset, the paper is between two relatively smooth rubber surfaces. If a web breaks in this unit, much damage can be caused. The paper tail can stick to the tacky inked surface of the plates or blankets and cause a wrap-up. There is no automatic way to open the nip so that a few layers will exert a very high pressure. *Smashed blankets* describes when a wad of paper crushes and embosses or permanently deforms the surface of a blanket. The same thing can happen to plates. Smashed plates and blankets also occur with DiLitho and web offset.

Printer to former

Many hundreds of feet of paper are in the press between the printing units and the former. The webs pass over many rollers in a very confusing way. They are slit and some leads go over angle bars or bay windows. Research has shown that nearly all web breaks start at the edge of a web from a nick or shive (5,6). Mechanical pulp is more apt to contain bundles of unseparated, unfibrillated fibers (i.e., shives), than chemical pulp. Good screening and cleaning is essential. There are many edges; for example, if eight full-width white rolls are webbed up, the operation starts with sixteen edges. They are all slit to half width or less which introduces at least sixteen more edges. The loss of any one web will stop the press. Frequently one web breaking will cause others to break. Cleaning up the waste paper on the press and rethreading a number of webs is very time-consuming, requires a lot of operators, and delays production.

If the paper has slack streaks or baggy edges, webs will not draw straight or they will tend to crease and wrinkle. If a slit is done on a slack streak, two baggy edges result.

The draws of all the webs must be controlled to a fraction of an inch so that the printed pages finish in register because they are cut off together. Tensions are maintained at about 2 pli but the paper must have uniform stretch characteristics not only from roll-to-roll, but across the web. When a web is slit, the resulting two webs must be the same. Beginning with unevenly wound rolls is going to compound the problems on a press.

Paper properties

Elasticity in newsprint is absolutely necessary. The paper is held firmly by the numerous printing units which are powered by a common drive. All the pages must come together precisely at the former and folder. The web leads are of varying lengths between the printing and collating stations. The webs vary in width as they progress. There must be a compensating factor—namely elasticity—to keep all the webs tight enough to be controlled. The webs are strained by the press and the stress in the web is a result. The lower the resulting stress from good stretch properties, the less chances of a web break (7). The stress at rupture is not a very useful number. Many properties which bear on runnability are enhanced by more moisture in the paper (Fig. 3.17, 3.18, 3.19, 3.20).

Fig. 3.17 illustrates how the ability of paper to stretch increases as the moisture content of the paper increases. Fig. 3.18 shows how the tensile strength decreases when the moisture content of paper is increased. A compromise must be met which is the moisture content at which the work-to-rupture is the maximum. It has been observed that the plots of Mullen tests at different moistures are very similar in shape to that of the plots of work-to-rupture at different moisture. Fig. 3.19 shows that different furnishes give different results, but there is always a moisture where the curve is maximum.

Studies of web breaks have shown that the vast majority are triggered by a fault from which a tear extends across the web. Internal tear strength resists this phenomenon. Fig. 3.20 illustrates how tear resistance is enhanced by higher moisture.

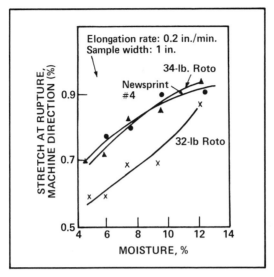

Fig. 3.17 Stretch at rupture vs. moisture (courtesy of Abitibi-Price, Inc.).

Paper considerations for printability

Publishers know what they like to see. A clean, sharp-looking job with good contrast gets a high rating. To achieve this, the blacks should be black and not speckled or gray, and the background should be as bright and white as possible without dirt specks. The background is not under the control of the printer, but he can improve the blackness and reduce the speckle to some degree by the printing method and by his manipulation of it. The paper is a limitation he cannot always overcome.

Stereo letterpress

In stereo letterpress, the ink is transferred to the paper surface from raised cast lead type. Dust is not a problem due to the deep relief and very heavy pressures to the point of embossing are used. A dark halo is usually cast around the edge of each letter while the center of dots and letters may be grayish. The blanket-covered impression cylinder compensates for major irregularities in the levelness of the plates. A compressible sheet of newsprint with moderate smoothness is needed.

Thin plate or shallow relief letterpress

In thin plate letterpress, the ink is transferred from a polymerized plastic surface. The relief is not as great as with stereos and dust can be a problem. Besides this drawback, the polymers are still under development and frequent-

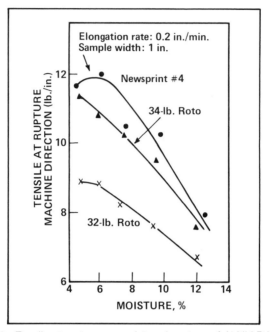

Fig. 3.18 Tensile at rupture vs. moisture (courtesy of Abitibi-Price, Inc.).

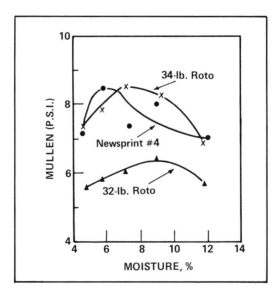

Fig. 3.19 Mullen vs. moisture (courtesy of Abitibi-Price, Inc.).

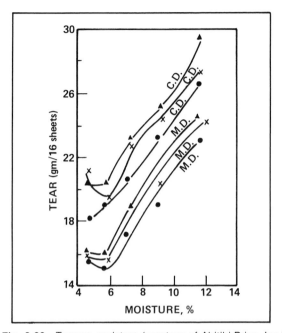

Fig. 3.20 Tear vs. moisture (courtesy of Abitibi-Price, Inc.).

ly the surface of the type tends to trap fibers and pull them out of the sheet. The platemaking department must have a good system of quality control. Curing of the plastic is critical so that it is hard enough but not brittle. The shape of the dots should be monitored with a microscope to be sure the shoulders are correct. Lighter pressures are used so press roller settings must be accurate; here the "kiss impression" is used. A much smoother sheet is needed than for stereo plates although cushion is still needed.

Lithographic processes

Offset lithography. Instead of raised surfaces to carry the ink, planographic or flat surfaces are used, and instead of the plate meeting the paper, the image is printed onto a rubber blanket and then to paper. The image on the plate is a chemical treatment which makes some areas of the plate water receptive and some ink receptive. Water transfers to the surface of the paper and the image is put on the paper from a flat surface; this makes a large difference to paper performance and to the appearance of the image.

The quality of printing from offset lithography is recognized to be the best obtained by any printing method. Denser, smoother solid areas, better dot fidelity, and a sharper appearance are obtained. There is no tendency for grayness in the center nor a halo at the edge of the letters. It takes skill and time on the part of the pressmen to get a proper balance between water and ink feed systems when a press starts, and until they do the printed newspapers are not salable. Usually, more waste is made each time the press is started than with letterpress printing. Web breaks mean stops and starts and therefore costs printed waste and down time.

Lint is the most difficult problem with offset. It is loosely bonded fibers, shives, and fines with no fibrillation to bond them. This debris from the paper surface accumulates on the blankets and distorts the printed image. At times, the press must be stopped and the blankets washed. If more than six grams of debris accumulate per square meter of blanket area through 20,000 impressions, frequent washups may be necessary; this depends on the job printed. A simple black and white format can run longer than some spot color or a three- or four-color process print. Well-trained press crews can reduce the lint problem a lot by skill and the choice of blankets and inks.

Since the printing is being done between two rubber surfaces, the process can tolerate fairly rough paper.

DiLitho. DiLitho is registered by ANPA/RI and is a shortened form for "direct lithography." The process does not have the intermediate rubber roll, so the metal lithographic plate prints directly onto the paper. It is a difficult system to control and maintain the ink-water balance because the absorbent newsprint takes ink from the plate and the water. More water must be fed to the plate than with offset to keep it clean and prevent linting. If there is not enough water, the ink travels to the nonprinting areas which causes the white areas of the page to turn gray.

DiLitho requires a very smooth paper with a lot of cushion. The image is put on from a flat metal surface, increasing the chances that the ink will not contact the micro-depressions in the surface. Few pressrooms are able to get offset quality.

Ink receptivity

Regular letterpress black is used with stereos, plastic plates, and DiLitho. Offset pressrooms use a more expensive offset ink. The ink must set by the vehicle soaking into the paper because there are no drying ovens on newspaper presses. For this reason, the paper must be uniformly absorbent. If areas do not absorb as well as adjacent areas, the ink film will appear mottled. From a papermaker's point of view, it seems that the phenomenon is a combination of formation, moisture, and calendering. Minute dense areas in the sheet are made even less absorbent by the pressure of the calender. If the moisture content is high, there is calender blackening. Blackening is a reduction in light-scattering capability which is related to porosity.

Ink showthrough

One of the excellent properties of stone groundwood pulp is that it imparts opacity to the paper. Publishers do not want to see the image from the back of a page discernible on the front. It is objectionable in editorial copy because it makes reading difficult, but cannot be tolerated in advertising where there may be large white areas. Unfortunately, actual opacity is only part of the problem. Standard news ink is made of about 12% carbon and the balance ink oil. Oil-soaked paper is transparent, so the ink lowers the opacity of the paper. Groundwood fines have high oil absorbtivity which helps to prevent the oil soaking completely through the sheet. Fillers tie up the oil but are not widely used because of cost. Strike-through occurs when the ink soaks through the sheet. Black specks appear if there are pinholes but otherwise the reverse side becomes dark with an oily appearance. The problem is increased by decreases in basis weight. The wedge print test is common for blackness and showthrough measurements.

Formation

Many printing problems are a direct result of poor formation. For example, 60-or 80-line screens are normally used for newspaper halftones. This means 60^2 or 80^2; i.e., 3600 or 6400 dots per sq. in.^{2}. For a smooth tone they must all be printed the same size and with the same amount of ink. This is not possible unless the formation is good and the voids in the surface are closed up or filled with fines. A single fiber in the sheet surface may be 0.0014 in. across. A halftone dot made by an 80-line printing plate etched to a 10% tone prints a dot of 0.0028 in. A space on the surface of a sheet of paper between fibers could be this size so a dot could be missed in printing. *Missing dots* describes the quality of printing and the number of dots is obtained by a count in a specified area.

Printing other than black and white

Color printing

While most newspapers are printed in black and white, more color is being used all the time. Publishers divide color work into two classes: advertising color and editorial color. Advertising color is sold to customers and is proven more effective than black and white and increases circulation. Editorial color, which is usually used for colored photographs on the front page, is paid for by the newspaper.

While photographs are often used in advertising, *spot color* is used extensively: areas of solid color which are laid up by hand on the pasteups from which the plates are made. Screens which will print uniform areas of dots for medium shades can also be put in by hand. Each color is printed on a separate printing couple with a special printing plate so web leads are made more complicated. When color printing is done on the press during the printing of a newspaper, it is referred to as ROP (run of press) to differentiate from preprinting. In 1979, 69% of newspapers reported printing color.

Color became more popular in newspapers when web offset was introduced. The system is ideally suited to process color. As of 1979, two-thirds of publishers use the four impressions (cyan, magenta, yellow, and black) while one-third do not use the black. This saves a printing unit but the picture is not quite as sharp.

Inserts

Newspapers of every size from community weeklies to metropolitan dailies and Sunday papers frequently contain inserts or "stuffers" which are put into the paper after it is printed on the regular press. They are nearly always of an advertising nature and range from small TV program guides with coated paper covers saddle stitched to multi-page newspaper-size colored flyers. On a large scale, inserts are relatively new and their use has been accelerated by the rapid increase in bulk mailing costs and the cost of door-to-door hand delivery. The existing distribution systems of the newspapers are vehicles to carry this material to the public.

The inserts, or *preprints*, are frequently the same in different newspapers: they are printed in an independent commercial shop, and delivered to the newspaper in bulk. The advertisers benefit by lower prices and better quality control; the scheduling need not be as rushed as it is for a daily paper. Some large publishers are setting up satellite printing plants but the bulk of the printing is done by other houses. The orders often run into millions of copies.

While some inserts are printed on newsprint, many are not. The groundwood specialty grades such as high bright rotonews, gravure papers, and machine coated are popular. A wide range of printing methods are also used, and the demand is high for spot or process color. The printing method and the paper choice are up to the advertiser.

In some of the larger newspapers the inserts or stuffers are put into the newspaper automatically. The fold in the newspaper is opened mechanically or with suction and the insert is fed in from a bin. The operation is much slower than the press so that several machines are needed to keep up with one press. Often there are multiple bins for a number of inserts into the same newspaper. Hand operation is still very common both at the newspaper and in the field. Often a large number of sections are sent to newspaper carriers to combine with the news section.

With the advent of color television, newspapers are in strict competition for the advertising dollar. Hence, the development of stuffers, a major source of income growth for newspapers.

Spectacolor

Printing either editorial color or advertisements ahead of time and rolling the job up in rolls identical in size to the rolls from the paper mills is called spectacolor. The rest of the paper is blank. When the picture is needed for an issue the roll is put on the press in the usual manner and black is printed in the blank areas and on the reverse side. The press must be equipped with a special sensing device and a tension control system to properly position the picture in relation to the printing cylinders. It has been found that the preprint must be printed about a 25 thousandth short so it can be stretched into register. To allow this, a moisture content of at least 8% is specified.

The preprinting process is most often gravure although web offset is sometimes used. The system was developed when stereos were still common as a way of introducing high quality color.

New developments

The methods of printing newspapers have changed radically in the last few years. The methods put specific demands on the paper; publishers now want paper for stereo, letterpress, offset, and DiLitho. The list will grow because there are more changes coming. Another is a new press being developed by ANPA using a new inking system and is called Anpapress. A number of systems convert stereo presses to run offset. Some are an extension of DiLitho by changing the web lead from the nip between the plate and the impression cylinder, allowing the image to be printed onto the blanket, and then transferring it to the paper in a new nip made by an extra roller. Others are a complete rebuild of the roller system. These systems will no doubt put other demands on the paper. The change from 32-lb newsprint (24 × 36-in. — 500) to 30-lb is relatively recent and 28-lb will be common soon. Opacity and showthrough will be even more important than they are at present.

Groundwood specialties

Many grades of paper that contain a high proportion of mechanical pulp are not printed in newspaper pressrooms. They are designed for special products and are frequently printed by commercial printers. Table 3.5 gives some typical ranges of weights and properties of these grades.

Catalogs

Most catalogs contain a large number of illustrations which must accurately and skillfully present and sell the merchandise. The choice of paper and printing process depends on the number of books, the type of merchandise, the size of the book, and the type of use expected of the publication. In some cases, such as women's apparel, precision in color is of the utmost importance. In other cases, simple illustrations in one color are sufficient. Merchandise prices vary so the price of printing and binding will vary. The cost of mailing or distribution is also a factor; the weight per unit usually must be limited.

Most catalogs are printed on paper that contains a high proportion of mechanical fiber. In many cases, clay coated paper is used, which may or may not be supercalendered. Clay coated sheets may contain up to 50% mechanical fiber and are used when high-fidelity color and good detail are needed. Less expensive uncoated papers with more mechanical fiber and machine finish or supercalendered serve well for a large volume of the business. Typical basis weights for uncoated catalog are 30 to 32 lb (24 × 36 in. − 500) (48.8 to 52.1 g/m^2) / (53.3 to 66.5 g/m^2) and for coated are 36 to 45 lb (25 × 38 in. − 500).

The covers for catalogs are frequently printed on heavy basis weight paper or board by sheet-fed offset presses. Covers are a special job and often are changed to suit regional distribution while the inner pages remain the same. The choice of cover stock and paper for the inner pages is made on the basis of how long the book will be in service, how frequently it might be used, and the environment in which it will be used. The same factors affect the system of binding.

Catalog binding

Saddle stitch. Double pages are folded in a V shape and collected (collated) on a bar with the cover on the top. Staples are driven down through the fold of the cover and inside pages and crimped on the inside. The system requires the paper to fold well and be strong enough that the staples do not tear out of the fold.

Perfect binding. Using a hot-melt plastic adhesive, single pages are stacked in the proper order and then clamped vertically so that the back of the book is horizontal and uppermost. A device automatically roughens all the edges where the glue is needed and a wheel applies a layer of molten plastic. The cover is wrapped around the body and adheres to the plastic along the back. The pages are only held in by the adhesive on the edge; the adhesive must be properly formulated and hot enough to get down into the fibers. This is more difficult with coated papers but can be very bothersome with all papers.

Loose leaf or with wire or plastic strip coil. A simple system requiring that the paper be punched along the backbone. Good punching characteristics and good tear are needed.

Table 3.5 Properties of mechanical fiber containers papers

	Newsprint	Roto News & Catalog	Offset	Directory	Paperback (pocketbook)
Basis weight (g/m²)	48.8	48.8 to 52.1	41.4 to 66.6	32.6 to 36.6	51.8 to 54.7
Caliper (mm)	.077 to .089	.063 to .076	.064 to .100	.052 to .060	.100 to .130
Gurley porosity (sec/100 ml)	15–50	70–130	30–70	25–50	40–60
Tear 16 sheets MD (mN) CD	125–175 190–230	145–178 180–240	140–170 190–260	100–150 160–210	195–295 295–395
Bendtsen roughness (ml/min)	90–200	20–90		50–80	60–200
Printsurf S10 (μm)	3.4–4.2	2.0–3.0	3.0–5.0	3.5–4.5	---
Mullen regular (kPa)	50–75	70–100	---	50–60	---
Stress at rupture (N/cm)	20–25	20–30	23–30	15–20	25–35
Strain at rupture MD (%)	0.9–1.2	0.9–1.1	0.9–1.2	0.8–1.0	---
Brightness (457nM) %	55–60	60–68	60–68	60	62.5
Printing opacity %	92–96	92–96	93–95	80–90	93–95
% Showthrough wedge 1.0 optical density	5–8	---	---	9–13	---
% Blackness wedge at 0.25 mil.	65–80	---	---	80–90	---
Larocque printability	64–69	---	---	---	---
Approximate mechanical pulp content	70–95	65–80	65–80	70–80	70–80

Printing methods for catalogs

Letterpress is no longer very popular in the big houses for printing catalogs. Web offset and roto (rotogravure) are used almost exclusively. Not long ago it was conventional to think that offset was good for short runs while gravure had to be used for long runs. The reasoning was that offset plate life was under 250,000 copies and gravure is good for millions. Offset plates have been greatly improved in recent years and many more copies can be printed with them. The plates are relatively inexpensive when compared to preparing a gravure cylinder and duplicates can be made quickly and easily.

The larger commercial printers frequently have various types and sizes of presses. Choosing the right press for the job depends on the volume of run; whether single-color, two-color, or four-color process is needed; what tonal quality the customer wishes; the price range of the job; and the grade of paper to use.

Web offset. The presses are basically the same as those described for newspapers except that drying ovens are located after each printing unit. The ovens are needed because the inks have a different formulation to news ink. They must gloss or shine by staying on the surface rather than by soaking in and therefore need energy to dry or harden. Slitting and folding are similar but more precise and the pages are much smaller as a rule. Runnability of the paper must be good. Press-stoppers caused by web breaks, creases, or jam-ups in the folder are very costly.

Uncoated papers need not be exceptionally smooth for offset printing but they must have a uniform surface. Uneven absorption of ink on the grades sold for catalogs is even more objectionable in these prints than in a newspaper. Finer tonal screens are used for catalog illustrations so lint can be even more of a problem than with newspapers. Excellent dimensional stability is very important when succeeding colors must be printed in perfect register.

Gravure. An uncomplicated printing method well suited for printing long catalog runs. While the engraved cylinders are expensive to prepare, they last a long time. There is little press make-ready since the cylinder runs in a fountain of ink with a doctor blade and the paper web is pressed against it with a rubber roller. Gravure offers two important advantages to the purchaser of catalog printing: it is capable of producing as wide a tone range as any other process and can do this on relatively inexpensive paper. Gravure also lends itself to scheduling; once the cylinders are made they can be lifted out of the press to make way for a more critical order and later returned to the press to complete the run with very little loss of production time. A major drawback of the method is the difficult page changes since the whole cylinder is etched in one operation. Current research on plastic sleeves for the cylinders and laser etching promises a reduction in cost and time while offering flexibility.

The printing presses are usually about 100 in. wide and often run only one web at a time. The solvent-based ink must be dried, and the solvent recovered, so each printing cylinder is followed by an oven. Only one color on one side can be printed at a time so there are often five units, four for printing process color and one for text. The web is then turned over with a bay window and fed through another five units. Slitters, formers, and folders are at the end of the line.

Single color or monotone may have a modified press arrangement. The paper chosen is frequently in the lower basis weight range of 24 to 30 lb (39.1 to 48.8 g/m^2), but it must have good opacity and ink strike-through resistance. It must also be very smooth and have as much cushion as possible. Good contact of every part of the paper surface to the cylinder is crucial. When a 100-line screen has been used to etch the cells, there are 10,000 cells per in.^{2}; if one fails to be touched by the paper, a dot is not printed and its absence is obvious to the eye.

Multicolor work is done on slightly higher basis weight paper which must be very smooth, have good cushion, be flat, and have very uniform caliper and dimensional properties. Excellent register of one color with the next which is printed on another unit is essential for a clean-looking print job.

Smoothness must be obtained without the sheet being crushed or blackened. The ink is picked out of the cells by absorption into the paper so the sheet also must be uniform. If it is not, the print will appear mottled with glossy and dull areas. Uniformity from roll to roll is most important in all respects to maintain register, to have uniform printing, and to keep colors and tone the same without mottle, speckle, and missed printing dots.

Directories

The most common directory is the telephone directory, which can range from a 6 × 9 in. saddle-stitched book of a couple of dozen pages to the 6.25 lb 9 × 12 in. perfect bound directories of larger U. S. cities. In the latter case, the classified section, or "yellow pages," is contained in a separate book of a size equal to the alphabetical directory.

In the past few years, the trend has been towards making the directory covers more attractive. Telephone companies are encouraging the subscribers to keep the directory handy and use it rather than call Information for an unfamiliar number. Particular care must be paid to the attractiveness of the classified section because different advertisers compete in the same directory. In the larger cities, the classified section shows better quality because the type for the alphabetical sections is revised frequently to produce traffic records (e.g. updated listings for switchboard use). Unit cost and accuracy for a directory is a major consideration to the purchaser.

Printing processes for directories

The trend in covers has been toward multicolor subjects on white stock, printed best by sheet-fed offset presses. It is common to print covers of identical design for many small cities within a telephone company's area, and then imprint the name of the city.

The text of directories is printed by letterpress using thin plates, or web offset. The web presses have rigid quality demands and require lighter basis weight paper than the presses for newspaper work. The normal basis weight of news at present is 30 lb (24 × 36 in. − 500) (48.8 g/m²) while 22.5 lb (36.6 g/m²) is the common basis for directory. Most purchasers of the catalog paper set very rigid minimum specification for opacity. Showthrough is also important and the caliper should be constant since it governs the thickness of the book.

Directories demand very clear, legible type, particularly since the individual letters are usually quite small. Offset gives the clearest impression and is good for the illustrations in the yellow pages. It originally had an advantage over letterpress because the plates are made photographically from cold composition (computers) while those for letterpress required hot lead. However, this advantage no longer applies since both plastic plates and DiLitho plates are also made photographically. In most cases letterpress and DiLitho are conversions of older, hot lead presses which is a transition situation until these presses are retired.

Paper requirements

Covers. Many directory covers are on white sheets. The southern mills, using bleached southern pulps, can supply white stock at a cheaper price than the former buff, gray, and green stocks commanded. As a result, a four-color job on the new white stock may cost the same as a single color on the tinted covers. Cover stocks should be strong, with good ink holdout, but open to a degree to facilitate ink drying. Good formation is important to assure even ink absorbency and thereby eliminate mottle. Cover stocks range in weight from 70 to 90 lb (20 × 26 in. − 500) (189 to 244 g/m²).

Text. The yellow pages can be considered a catalog. Advertisers want to see their illustrations properly and clearly reproduced. It is possible that color will be used in the future. Offset is excellent for this work since it does not demand a particularly smooth paper. When letterpress or DiLitho is used both smoothness and cushion or bulk are needed.

Opacity and lack of ink strike-through and showthrough are of paramount importance on the yellow pages and on the white pages. Good formation and the absence of pinholes are needed as well as carefully balanced calendering to get smoothness without loss of opacity. Color and brightness should be uniform from roll to roll of paper supplied since a change in shade is readily visible on the edge of a book and detracts from its appearance. Lint is even more undesirable with catalog than it is with news. Offset is particularly susceptible to lint problems; even letterpress, unless the plates are very well made, can be spoiled.

Binding. Perfect binding is generally used for books of more than 1/4 to 3/8 in. thick. Otherwise, side stitching is used with the cover glued over the stitching. For very small books saddle stitching is used. The text paper for saddle-stitched books is of a higher basis weight to maintain sufficient strength that the center pages will not pull out of the stitches. For all books, the grain is optional except for the cover. The cover should be printed grain long and bound with the grain parallel to the backbone.

Paperbacks or pocket books

The paperback book has become very popular in the last few decades. Novels and classics, traditionally case bound in hardcovers are reprinted in paperback and many texts and technical books are now originally printed and sold this way. The paper used is a heavyweight mechanical pulp-based sheet which is somewhat thicker and stiffer than newsprint. Such names as Novel News, Bulky News, and Paperback are used by the mills to identify it. Basis weights are about 35 to 37 lb. (24 × 36 in. – 500) (57 to 60 g/m^2). The caliper is as high as 0.005 in., and must be held to close tolerance so that the thickness of the book does not vary.

One method of printing and binding uses a special press that prints paperbacks in a unique way. One whole book is printed, collated and perfect bound in one cycle of the machine. The machine consists of a flexible conveyor belt onto which are glued a set of individual page plastic letterpress printing plates. The conveyor belt, together with a web of paper, is passed between two rollers to press the plates, which have been inked, against the sheet. The web is thus printed with one impression of each odd-numbered page. When the reverse side is printed the same way with the even pages the web goes to slitters, folders, and a collator which puts them together in the proper sequence. A cover is attached during the perfect binding operation; one complete book is printed in one cycle.

Supercalendered newsprint

Gravure is very popular in Europe for magazines and similar products. Supercalendered uncoated paper is most often used. Recently there have been developments in Finland to make supercalendered newsprint. The paper has found favor in North America, mostly for gravure, and now a number of North American mills are equipped with supercalenders for this market. The sheets made in Europe are often highly filled, whereas most in North America are not.

Publication papers

The printing methods discussed to this point have all been for webs with paper easily identified as containing groundwood or mechanical fiber. A grade that is not as easily identified, yet contains approximately 50% mechanical fiber is light weight coated (LWC). Magazines with many four-color process pictures and advertisements look much better printed on coated paper. The surface is smoother and more glossy, and the ink stays on the surface. Drying ovens are needed to cure the ink and prevent smearing. Letterpress, offset lithography, and gravure are used to print but modifications are made to the coating.

The basis weight of LWC is usually in the 34 to 36 lb (50.3 to 53.3 g/m^2) range although some mills make heavier sheets. The coating is done on the paper machine, usually with trailing blade coaters, which apply coat weights in the 3.5 to 5 lb per side range. The brightness is about 68 to 70 for an average sheet of this No. 5 grade.

Groundwood web offset and offset

Stone groundwood is the least expensive fiber and sheets that contain it have a price edge over free sheets. Now groundwood and the new refiner-made fiber can be bleached so the trend is to make brighter sheets containing these fibers. Office papers in the 15 to 18 lb (17 × 22 in. − 500) (56.4 to 67.7 g/m^2) are marketed with a brightness of 70. Offset (sheeted paper for sheet-fed presses) and web offset are also made to this brightness. These are classed as No. 1 quality on the brightness and opacity scale. When these brighter sheets are used for coating base, the coated paper also comes up in the scale.

Word processors, office copiers, and computer printers are becoming commonplace. They use a great deal of paper and cutting costs is essential. Bonds, register, and manifold papers, which are free sheets, were used initially; however, interest in using groundwood-containing papers has risen particularly for copies that do not require much handling or long storage life.

Literature cited

1. Victor Strauss, "The Printing Industry" 1967, p. 225 Pub. by Printing Industies of America, Inc.
2. S. M. Hussain, W. R. Farrell, J. R. Gunning. *Canadian Pulp and Paper Industry* 21 (8):52 (1968).
3. S. M. Hussain and W. R. Farrell, TAPPI 60(5):112 (1977).

4. R. G. Lucas, "Internal Gearing in a Roll of Paper," paper presented at TAPPI Finishing Conference, Asheville, N. C. October 7-10, 1974.
5. G. R. Sears, R. F. Tyler, C. W. Denzer, *Pulp and Paper Magazine Canada*, 66(7):T351 (1965).
6. F. A. MacMillan, W. R. Farrell, K. G. Booth, *Pulp and Paper Magazine Canada*, 66(7):T361 (1965).
7. J. R. Gunning, *TAGA Proceedings*, 1965, p. 137.

Section IV
Coated Grades and Commercial Printing

W.P. Greenwood and A.S. Taylor, Editors

8
Box Wrap Papers

J. Pinder

Introduction

Box wrap papers comprise a broad category of specialty papers. The historical development of decorative box wrap papers, both uncoated and coated grades, is associated with the development of other papers used in gluing applications, i.e., label papers and wallpapers. A large variety of papers are used as box wraps and other applications, including note pad covers, menu covers, desk calendars, novelty items, photograph mounts, game backs, shelf paper, and applications involving minimum use furniture and carrying cases. The availability of many types of plastics in recent years has meant that box wrap papers are concentrating more and more in areas where their uniqueness relating to color, texture, glueability, and printing performance are recognized and less in areas where specific performance requirements exist which may be better satisfied with nonpaper products.

Box wrap papers are mainly employed with set-up boxes. These are glued, rigid boxes and are distinct from folding boxes. Folding boxes are being largely supplied by conventionally printed fourdrinier and multiformer produced boxboard, both uncoated and coated.

Uncoated box wrap papers

Uncoated box wrap papers normally comprise beater-dyed kraft papers, which are usually machine glazed, often are water marked, are increasingly embossed, and in special cases are design printed.

Coated box wrap papers

Conventional coated box wrap papers are produced mainly by aqueous air-knife coating processes. The coating operation is normally followed by one or more operations of supercalendering, gloss calendering, friction calendering, printing, print-embossing, and embossing. Some box wrap papers are produced by solvent coating and the gravure process is widely preferred, as it is well suited to controlled application of the colored coatings.

Coated box wrap papers include papers of a wide range of quality: high gloss, suede finish, metallic and embossed. The more expensive and higher quality grades are multicoated and often are considered to excel in specific attributes. Cast coated papers, for example, exhibit high gloss and very uniform surface appearance. These papers are available as plain and lacquered papers in a full range of colors. At the opposite end of the quality spectrum are lightly coated stocks in which a limited improvement in properties such as water resistance, durability, and gloss may be revealed by comparison to uncoated grades.

The physical and appearance properties of paper which are important for box wrap purposes largely determine the paper used. One of the most important physical properties concerns uniform dimensional stability, particularly as this relates to freedom from curl. In order to minimize curl, stocks of a porous nature, including groundwood containing stocks, have traditionally been preferred. Because box wrapping involves gluing generally with water base glues, the gluing and adhesive related characteristics of the paper are very important. The papers must conform readily to the box shapes during manufacture and drying of the glue. The interior and underside of the paper must be similar in color to the surface of the paper so that box fold and overlap portions will be inconspicuous. The importance of appearance is best understood from analyzing uses for perfume boxes and jewelry boxes such as creating a positive impression of the often relatively expensive article contained in the box to the buying public. Those characteristics which are controlled especially to enhance a pleasing appearance include: color, gloss, texture, and resistance to discoloration from scuffing or staining. For non-box wrap applications such as photograph mounts, desk calendars, backs of games, and covers for notebooks, the end use performance properties of other than gluing and appearance-related properties receive greater emphasis. These additional properties concern mainly strength properties: fold strength, tear resistance, and surface abrasion resistance.

In recent years increased attention has been given to increasing the light fastness and water resistance of box wrap papers. Light fastness is of particular importance in display applications and in applications involving durable items. Water resistance must be of a minimum level so boxes exposed to moisture during handling will resist deteriorating enough not to contaminate counter tops, clothing, or other articles with which boxes might come in contact in normal use.

Traditionally, box wrap papers have been printed by letterpress and silk screen printing techniques, with a minor amount of foil stamping. In recent years, offset lithography and to a lesser degree flexography have been used increasingly for printing. The change to offset lithography from letterpress has necessitated improved control of the water resistance characteristics of the papers and has introduced new tolerances on the abrasive nature of the papers. The trend to increased use of offset lithography results in printers judging traditional box wrap papers by comparison with coated and uncoated white offset stocks. Box wrap papers are favored since print coverage is often small and run sizes usually are small by comparison to run sizes with white stocks. An exception to this generalization occurs in pastel-colored label stocks, coated and uncoated, in which some traditional box wrap papers have been replaced by offset colored stocks. With some of these stocks the printing performance is fully comparable to that of the white stocks.

Box wrap papers have often simulated the appearance of natural products: wood, textiles, and leather. Woodgrains and leather appearances are well simulated through combinations of colors, prints, and emboss patterns. Because the paper products are readily adaptable to producing novelty variations and leather is expected to remain in relative scarcity, the future for this category of papers is bright.

9
Label Papers

N. Kinley

Introduction

Most label papers can be categorized into either coated or uncoated book papers. These papers are either gummed or ungummed and are printed by offset, gravure, letterpress, and sometimes flexography. The following are the most commonly used label papers:

Cast coated, one side paper. Cast coated paper is made by allowing the coating to dry on the paper web while in intimate contact with a highly polished casting surface such as a large internally-heated chromium-plated drum. This produces a coated paper with a very high gloss and an extremely smooth surface. These are used where label printing requires a broad spectrum of toning and where a superb printing job is required.

Coated one side papers #1 and #2. Air-knife coated papers that have bright color and good opacity with a variety of finishes: matte, dull, or high gloss. They are made for offset and letterpress reproduction of fine screen halftones. The uncoated side of these papers is rough and designed for pasting.

#3 coated one side papers. By far the most popular grade, this sheet is coated one side book and also termed label paper (letterpress) or coated one side label paper litho. Some are designed for offset but can be used for letterpress printing as well. However, letterpress coated papers are usually unsuited for offset equipment because the starch binders used for letterpress grades would tend to pick. Some letterpress papers are particularly adapted for varnishes and for gloss or metallic inks. This grade, whether letterpress or litho, is used for the broad market of can labels, jar labels, posters, and many other uses, particularly in the food industry.

Uncoated papers. These papers have a medium smooth surface obtained from the calender stack on the dry end of the papermaking machine. Machine finish (MF) book is a relatively inexpensive general utility paper and usually available to the trade in five different grades. The quality of the paper is determined by grade and the properties; the sheet may be altered to meet the needs of the ultimate users. For example, MF book can be used for halftones up to 110-line screen, but 100-line is usually the maximum. Some MFs go beyond 85-line screen. A supercalendered finish (SF) or English finish (EF) is required for printing halftones of 120- to 133- line screen. It is the quality of printing that generally determines the grade used. As indicated, uncoated book is a variable in various rates and finishes: machine finish, MF; English finish, EF, which is a high machine finish; and supercalendered, SC, which is a separate operation. Uncoated papers are generally used for more simple line work and often for text only.

Characteristics of label papers

Appearance. Appearance sells the product. If the label is well designed, if the color scheme is pleasing to the customer, and if the color reproduction is sharp and bright so a positive, image-building visual impression is conveyed to the customer, then the silent salesman, the label, will sell the product. To the lithographer and to his customer appearance means:

1. No blemishes caused by hickeys.
2. No wet rub.
3. No scratches.
4. White areas complete clean.
5. Margins even.
6. Image square and in correct position to match up on the lap.
7. Glueability of the paper surface such that the label will not come off the can.
8. Consistency of color for mass display purposes. Consistency of color whether the paper and the lithographing was done this month, last month, this year or next year.

How can the papermaking process, the papermaker, and the lithographer work together to give the end user a quality label?

Would you buy an apple with a worm hole in it? Would you wear a white shirt with a blotch on it? These questions are asked so as to put into perspective the food packager's aversion to spots or "hickeys." If the can label depicts applesauce, then a hickey on the full color apple illustration suggests poor quality to the consumer. And because all fruits and vegetables are graded for quality according to freedom from blemishes, the packer of the food product does not want the label or package to have blemishes or hickeys.

The greatest source of spoilage in a paper and boxboard converting plant is caused by hickeys. Because of hickeys, thousands of dollars worth of finished goods otherwise suitable for shipping are scrapped and baled and sent back to the mill. Mills using reclaimed materials see tons of cartons returned to be recycled and used in the backliner of boxboard.

Loose particles, pieces coming out of the surface, or blistering are common sources of hickeys. The lithographer tries to eliminate the loose particles by equipping his press with a high vacuum sheet cleaner. One sheet cleaner uses a precision high roller covered with a special covering. When rotated, the roller causes the fibers to stand up by centrifugal force to remove any loose fiber or coating dust by the vacuum exhaust system. Poorly bonded specks or shives which are not removed by the sheet cleaner are sometimes pulled from the sheet at the nip between the press blanket and the sheet. To get around this plucking problem, the lithographic pressman reduces the tack of his inks. There are limits to which a pressman can go with reducing inks; printing quality on multicolor presses depends on inks trapping subsequent inks in the printing process. For good trapping demands tacky first down inks. The lithographer also uses special hickey-picking rolls, such as the rodel roller, which has a fine leather-like nap. The hickey-picking roller is set with a minimum stripe, so the roller nap flicks the hickey from the plate to the next above roller and then transfers back up into the roller train.

Teflon-covered rollers are also used for hickey picking. With these rollers there is a high degree of electrostatic energy attraction, which pulls the hickey from the plate to be run and is then transferred into the roller train.

Higher press speeds and higher tack inks on five- and six-color presses create the need for papers with adequate surface strength. But in many instances the lithographer is running his press slower than normal to suit the inadequate surface strength of the paper. Improvements are needed in the ink receptivity of the paper surface and in lithographic inks and blankets for the ink film to split more readily, enabling faster press speeds.

In earlier times when casein was the principal ingredient in coated papers, the term "milking" was used to describe the lack of bonding strength in the coating formulation. The clay separated from the sheet and adhered to the blanket when the sheet was pressed at the nip between the blanket and the impression cylinder of the lithographic press. This clay dust would build up to a point where it severely affected the print quality and the pressman would have to wash the blanket. Sometimes a making of paper could be saved through frequent washings of the blanket. Other times the paper would have to be rejected as unsuitable for lithographic printing. With the advent of latex binders in the coating formulation, the problem is now infrequent.

Proper registration. Lithographers are puzzled when on press the images on a five-color press are registering perfectly and the pressman puts in a skid of the same grade and size of the paper from the same mill and instantly the printed image goes out of register. Back edge stretch apparently due to stresses and tensions caused at the blanket nip seem greater in some makings of paper; the stretch may be due to the furnish used and to the sheet formation made by the particular paper machine. After making adjustments to the press the second sheet usually can be run satisfactorily.

When the lithographer has a form with solid areas followed by white areas, the difference in elasticity plus differences in blanket release properties of the sheet will occasionally result in a printed sheet in the delivery of the press tending to waffle. To remedy the condition, the lithographer can reduce the tack of inks, reduce printing pressures to a minimum, and reduce the speed of the press. Occasionally, waffling can be so severe that it will result in curly labels from all areas of the sheet when the printed sheets are cut in the guillotine.

Other times the stresses will produce creases in the gripper to back edge direction, particularly when the moisture content of the paper is out of balance with the relative humidity of the pressroom. Conditioning the paper will sometimes help this problem.

Years ago, the standard basis weights for label papers was 25×38 in. 140M (140 lb/1000 sheets). Then 120M was thought to be the minimum which was compatible with good papermaking and lithographing. Now some 110 lb/1000 weight is being used and requests for 100M are occasionally encountered. If the nature of the finished printed result is simple, such as a light form with small areas of type without the need for heavy solids or the trapping of wet ink films on wet ink films on four- or five-color presses, then these lightweight papers can sometimes be used successfully. But if the quality requirement is high, it is in the best interest of the papermaker and the lithographer that basis weight 120 lb/1000 be used.

Aside from distortion of the sheet which causes register variation, the lithographer often runs into back edge hook, which is most pronounced in lightweight papers. One maker's paper in the same grade and weight will run satisfactorily and another maker's will not. The nature of the fiber used in the base stock, the formation of the sheet, the density of the sheet, and the release properties of the coated surface seem to affect this tendency to back edge hook. To get the sheet through the press, the lithographer can reduce press speed, reduce the tack of his inks, and reduce printing pressure to where the solid image is almost breaking.

Inking. Variations in coating smoothness show up in solids on the printed sheet. Cyan, in particular, will show coating streaks. These bad coatings give a "mealy" result in the finished job and are very difficult for the lithographer to spot ahead of time. Almost anyone can spot poor printing results once ink has been put on paper but almost none can visually inspect paper and predict how the sheet will perform on the press and how it will print. But once ink is put on paper, it is largely the responsibility of the converter to prove to the paper manufacturer the paper's possible defects. The wise converter establishes and maintains an effective understanding and working relationship with the paper company technical service man so that they can work together on paper-press problems.

The physical properties of the paper surface such as absorbtivity, ink holdout, and smoothness have quite a bearing on the setting of inks and on the finished reproduction. The ink manufacturers have developed new quick-setting inks with the objective that the inks be touch dry in the pile within minutes after printing. These inks enable the lithographer to run small piles of several thousand sheets on coated stocks on solid forms which would have required racking in 500s not so long ago.

The ink suppliers have also created low tack ink which will trap wet film on wet films at much lower tack forces than used even a few years ago. High-speed sheet-fed presses running up to 7500 sheets per hour need the assist of these low tack inks to split the sheets from the blanket. Inks matched to paper surface or paper matched to the latest quick-set inks are needed by the lithography industry.

White is a color. This is sometimes overlooked in color reproduction. The blueness, the pinkness, and the creaminess of the paper coating will throw the cast color in one direction or another. Food subjects in which green is objectionable because of the association of green mold are usually best run on paper stocks with a slightly cream white cast. Designs that are predominately blue will reproduce better on blue white coatings which complement their colors.

If a paper company has been manufacturing a paper with a certain color of white, it should advise the lithographer of any change. And if the lithographer is buying his paper from a jobber he should specify one make. If different makes of paper are mixed in a run, then there will be changes in the color reproduction.

Variations in ink absorbtivity and ink holdout will cause an ink to dry up or down. Dark green, strong browns, in fact, any saturated colors made from large tonal percentages of the process colors will dry differently if the paper is absorbent. An exaggeration of this condition would be if the lithographer ran a coated stock and then used an uncoated stock. He would get a much different result.

The ink maker tries to match a given color with a surface absorptivity and ink holdout which varies from run to run and within the run. The paper-maker tries to supply a reasonably consistent product in which is applied an ink which varies considerably from ink maker and which varies according to the skills of the lithographer. The lithographer tries to bring together these materials to turn out a consistent product which will satisfy the statistical quality control requirements of the end user. A problem for both paper and ink manufacturers in terms of product goes back to naturally run materials. The lithographer has an unsuitable process which is affected by these materials. The degree of ink emulsification varies considerably and depends on the ink and on the lithographer's skills.

Papermakers, ink manufacturers, and lithographers need to establish quality guidelines to help each other do a better job and please the end user. Tremendous waste is created by each industry due to the lack of knowledge and understanding between industries.

10
Noncellulose Papers

B.M. Wood and E. Anczurowski

Introduction

Over the past ten or fifteen years considerable technical effort has been directed toward developing noncellulosic (synthetic) papers. Basically, two approaches have been used to produce paper-like structures from synthetic polymers: extrusion of a film from a low cost polymer and the formation of a sheet from synthetic fibers. Papers produced from films are called *film-based synthetic papers* and papers produced from synthetic fibers are called *fiber-based synthetic papers*.

Film-based synthetic papers

The most common raw materials used in film-based papers are low and high density polyethylene, polypropylene, polyvinyl chloride and polystyrene. The manufacture of plastic papers involves three main steps: forming a plastic sheet, stretching the film, and paperizing (a treatment to produce paperlike properties).

The plastic sheet is formed from polymer pellets by extrusion, calendering, or casting. As the next step, the film is stretched biaxially to improve its mechanical properties, e.g. tensile, tear, strength, and stiffness. The plastic films are then paperized. The aim of paperizing is ensure sheet opacity and provide a surface with good printability. Paperization can be achieved either on the surface only or throughout the whole sheet. Surface paperization involves: surface treatment with a solvent, chemical, or flame; mechanical or electronic (Corona discharge) methods; or coating with clays, resins, or resin containing filler. Bulk paperization can be achieved by forming the plastic or by the compounding of plastics with fillers or plastic mixtures.

The advantages of film-based synthetic papers include a high burst strength, folding endurance, elongation, and dimensional stability. The drawbacks of film-based synthetic papers are low heat resistance, poor basestock opacity, broke recovery in their manufacture, some printing and converting problems, disposal difficulties, and high cost.

Film-based paper end uses include book covers, tag and pressure sensitive labels, notion and shopping bags, and shrink, blister, and skin packages.

Fiber-based synthetic papers

The other route to paper-like products from synthetics is through the formation of a sheet from fibers, which can be produced by the extrusion of polymers (spunbonded products), from synthetic fibers, or from synthetic pulp in the papermaking process.

Spunbonded synthetic papers. The papers are classified as continuous filament, fibrous structures produced in a process which is integrated with fiber manufacture. They are produced by *flash spinning*, which is an extrusion of soluble or fusable polymers through very fine nozzles at high speeds. High velocity air (2 miles a minute) eliminates undesirable "molecular chain folding." Success in the process requires that the filament be oriented, while being extruded and laid in the tacky state, to a uniform web of continuous fiber. The web is then flattened and pressed into sheets by heat and pressure.

Spunbound products combine properties of fabrics, films, and papers. Toughness and puncture resistance are outstanding. The combination of high nondirectional tensile strength, tear strength, and flex is also unique. Spunbonded materials, when coated, give excellent printability. End use application for spunbonded include tags, banners, labels, charts, maps.

Papers from short synthetic fibers. The papers are produced from a dilute suspension on conventional or modified paper machines such as the Rotoformer and the inclined wire fourdrinier. Laying synthetic fiber webs from foam media or by the dry-forming route is also possible and is especially desirable in the case of hydrophobic fibers.

The most common artificial fibers used in papermaking are polyamides (nylons), polyester, acrylics, polyvinyl acetates, polyvinyl alcohols, glass, and asbestos. Artificial fibers for use in papermaking are cut to a short length [1/8-1 in. (3.2 mm-25.4 mm)] to produce acceptable formation. The exact length depends on the *denier*, a textile unit related to the diameter of fiber.

Bonding of the synthetic fiber web is a key problem. Generally, man-made fibers cannot be bonded as a result of mechanical action in water, which is necessary with the usual cellulosic raw materials (wood fiber) in papermaking. Bonding systems for artificial fibers can be divided into two classes: self-bonded and externally bonded. The polymer industry has succeeded in producing self-bonding fibers: fibrillatable fibers which are processed and bonded similarly to wood fiber, and bicomponent synthetic fibers in which the thermoplastic bonding is achieved by melting the outer shell consisting of a low melting point polymer. Bonding can be achieved by treating fibers with solvents. In the external systems, bonding is derived from added binders in the form of thermoplastic fibers, fibrids, polymer emulsions, and polymer solutions. The most common fibrous binders are those produced from thermoplastic polymers. Fibrids are polymeric structures produced by special solution polymerization techniques. The most common polymers in water-based emulsions are polyacrylates, polyvinyl acetates, polybutadiene, polyacrylonitrile copolymers, polyvinyl chloride, and polyvinyl acetates. Such polymers are supplied in a wide range of compositions and include materials ranging from soft and rubbery to stiff and hard. Water-based emulsions are used most widely because of their relatively low cost, great variety, and ease of application. Solvent solutions are less frequently used because of difficulties in working with solvents.

A number of the available synthetic fibers and binders offer opportunities for designing products to meet particular end uses. The strength of synthetic papers can be several times that of conventional papers. High dimensional stability, good electrical resistance, and other specific properties can be developed by proper selection of fibers and binders. The most common applications for synthetic fiber papers are filters, tea bag paper, wall coverings, and packaging materials.

So far, the relatively high cost of 100% synthetic fiber papers has prevented significant inroads, except in specialty products. However, remarkable progress has recently been made in developing grades of polymer fiber/wood fiber blends. These are now manufactured in commercial amounts on commercial paper machines.

Papers from synthetic pulp. Recently, the development of synthetic pulp has attracted a great deal of attention. This fibrous polymeric product can be processed as wood pulp on the conventional paper machines. It is bright, gives good opacity, and can be mixed with wood fibers to produce paper grades of varying qualities and characteristics.

Disposable synthetic papers

One of the main drawbacks of papers produced from polymeric materials is disposability. Plastics by their very nature are chemically inert. However, new degradable polymers have been developed. Additives cause decomposition in the polymers by a photo-oxidative chain mechanism triggered by light. As the polymer degrades, it is further attacked by common microorganisms.

Water-soluble synthetic papers are another answer to ecology problems. These papers are produced from polyvinyl alcohol and methylcellulose. The papers look and act like conventional papers and can be printed and coated. End uses include, among others, packaging products and pressure sensitive "dissolve-away" labels.

Cellulosics for labels and packaging are continuously being challenged by improved plastic papers (films), fiber paper, or paper combined with cellulosics. It is not always the initial cost that determines the kind that will be used in a particular package. However, in spite of these challenges, synthetics will continue to be used for new and conventional products where special characteristics justify their extra cost.

Section VI
Book Publishing Papers
W.H. Bureau, Editor

11
Book Publishing Papers

W.H. Bureau

Introduction

Paper requirements for book manufacturing fall into two broad, overlapping categories: aesthetic or appearance characteristics and printability–runnability characteristics. The latter affects the print quality and/or mechanical and physical factors which in turn determine the ability of the web or sheet to withstand and not be affected by the stresses placed upon it by the printing press. The two requirements usually are set by the paper customer in the form of paper specifications and sent to the mill as part of the purchase agreement. Major book publishers tend to select a specific sheet when launching a new series of titles. Frequently trial printings on a variety of available papers are made. Once selected, a grade may be used for a period of years.

The printer normally has nothing to do with paper selection and may or may not be aware of the exact paper specifications as ordered. However, he rightfully expects to receive a sheet of paper that minimizes printing problems, both mechanical (i.e., getting the paper through the press) and in the subjective area of print quality. Original design concepts can influence many subsequent steps in book manufacture. For example, is gloss ink brilliance desired or not? If so, then the printer needs a paper that will enable him to obtain this result. The printer should not be in a position of trying to develop sharp print quality on paper not suited for that purpose. To help ensure that incoming paper meets minimum requirements in printability and runnability, the printer subjects the stock to a series of paper quality control tests. In some cases, the paper is compared to standard specifications to ensure uniformity from mill run to mill run and uniformity within a mill run.

Aesthetic or appearance characteristics

Color
Color in book publishing papers normally ranges from a blue-white to a natural shade. It is important to hold color consistent throughout the run;

otherwise the book will turn out *stripped*: signatures of varying shades that appear in the book as dark and light sections. Stripping occurs because in the construction of a book, adjacent signatures (groups of pages) are produced from paper literally miles apart on the paper machine, showing drifting shade as an abrupt color change. Shade drift is magnified by *edge stain*, an aniline dye used to stain the edges of a book for decorative purposes. Publishers will select a specific shade which they will use repeatedly for a series of books over a period of years. Inventories of paper are sometimes maintained for a series of books, and new deliveries are expected to match past deliveries. Color measuring instruments are used increasingly to match shade and maintain color standards. The *colorimeter* automatically takes a reflectance reading through a series of filters and numerically defines the color of paper on a three-dimensional scale whose units are know as L, a, and b.

A definite pastel paper color is utilized with a coordinated ink color for some books. For example, a green pastel or tinted paper may be used with a brown ink for ease of reading.

Brightness

Brightness is important, especially when working to a standard. Brightness contributes to the subjective grading of printability, probably in the area of contrast. If two sheets are equal in all respects except brightness, the higher brightness will usually be judged superior. GE brightness is not used alone as a test measurement of the appearance of paper since it tells only the reflectance of paper at a wavelength of 457 nanometers. Actually, two sheets of paper can be the same brightness and yet be much different in appearance. For this reason, both brightness and color tests are used to measure the appearance of paper.

Gloss

Gloss is the ability of paper to reflect light rays. Gloss is a matter of choice. Some desire a glossy product; others, a dull one. In some cases, the desired result is a glossy ink on a dull sheet. High paper gloss distracts from reading and is often objectionable. The National Association of State Textbook Administrators (NASTA) specifications for textbooks specify a maximum permissible gloss for this reason.

Texture

Texture varies from supercalendered to antique finish. Special finishes such as felt marked and laid finishes may be used. Texture may be selected to help establish the mood for the reader. Often, however, finish is of secondary importance since book publishing papers are manufactured to bulk.

Opacity

Opacity, or light-stopping ability, is very important. A paper low in opacity lets the printing on the back side show through, greatly affecting the attractiveness and legibility of the printed product. Low opacity can ruin a perfect printing job. Opacity becomes more important in lighter basis weights, i.e., under 50 lb. Actually, the combined effects of insufficient opacity and lack of ink holdout can result in very unsatisfactory final apparent opacity, especially for 40 and 45 lb basis weights.

Defects

Defects such as dirt, holes, streaks, grease spots, scratches, and even hand and foot prints are not very attractive, and in some cases affect printability and runnability.

In summary, appearance is very important. Appearance factors are mostly subjective but are expected to remain uniform once selected for the sheet.

Printability/runnability characteristics

The second requirement category for book manufacturing as mentioned before is printability–runnability. Many factors affect the ability of the printer to produce a satisfactory product with a reasonable amount of effort and cost, including:

1. Failure of the sheet to hold its size and shape through the press, resulting in wrinkles, misregister, doubling, slurring, etc.
2. Strength requirements as related to tearing, stretching, bursting, bending, and folding stresses.
3. Strength requirements as related to the surface and internal bonding strength of the sheet to avoid blanket contamination, delamination, and blisters.
4. Cleanliness requirements relating to foreign material in the load: slitter dust, lint, scale—anything on the surface of the sheet loose enough to be picked up by the tacky blanket ink combination and subsequently released into the ink train of the press.
5. Variation in slipperiness can cause folder jam-ups. Paper that is too slippery causes folder variation and handling problems after printing.
6. Out-of-square paper when trimming causes misregister and complicates further bindery work, which requires two straight edges at right angles for register guides.
7. Good mechanical roll conditions is one of the most important factors in any web-fed printing operation. If, because of calender cuts, bursts,

wood shives, cracked edges, mill pasters, fiber cuts, slime holes, slack area, poor winding, etc., the paper cannot be put through the press, it makes little difference whether the paper is printable or not.

Printing processes and paper selection

The three main printing processes are *letterpress*–sheet-fed or web, and the Cameron Belt Press; *gravure*–sheet-fed and web; and *offset* or *lithography*–sheet-fed and web. The processes differ mainly in the physical characteristics of the printing plate and therefore differ in their demands upon printing paper.

Letterpress

Letterpress requires a relatively smooth, level sheet but not as smooth as required for gravure. Resistance to picking is also important but less demanding than offset. The higher the printing quality (halftones and four-color work), the more demanding is the process for smooth and level paper. Letterpress can print up to a 110-line screen on smooth, level, English finish uncoated papers. Letterpress screens of 120 lines or finer per inch require an enamel coated surface.

The Cameron Belt Press, as shown in Fig. 11.1, is typical letterpress printing in image transfer. It is unique with respect to the number of printing plates and the manner in which they are attached. Instead of plates for a proportional part of the total number of pages (32, 64, 128, etc.) attached to a flat bed or cylinder, all the plates are affixed to two endless belts that print a complete book in their one revolution. The web is slit into ribbons one or two pages wide, chopped into two- and/or four-page signatures, gathered into complete books, and fed directly into a perfect binder.

The Cameron Belt Press paper requirements may be the most demanding of all processes. It requires the smoothness and levelness of letterpress, surface strength approaching that of offset (heat-set inks and gas flame dryers are used), the roll perfection of web offset, and much tighter caliper control.

Since the Cameron Belt Press prints a complete book for each revolution of the belt, this means a complete book is printed on each corresponding length of paper. Minor variations in caliper cause major differences in the bulk of the book since complete books are produced on each caliper extreme: thin books from low caliper and thick books from high caliper. In the binding operation, covers (either casebound or paper) are made to fit a particular bulk. If the bulk varies, the covers may be too small or too large and undesirable books are produced. In printing operations producing signatures, the thin and thick signatures are so intermingled within the book they tend to offset each other and produce a book of average bulk.

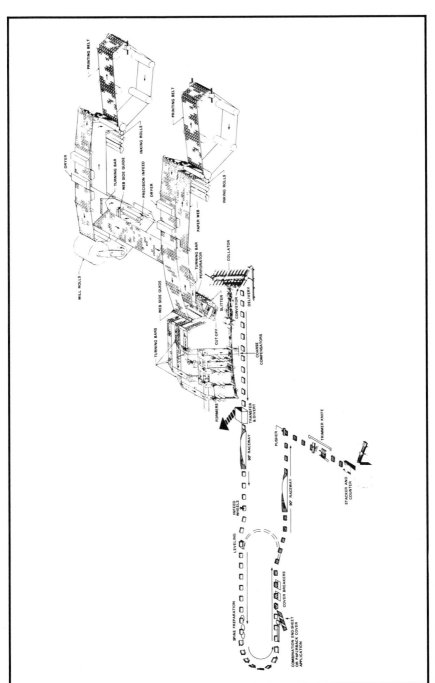

Fig. 11.1 Cameron Belt press.

Letterpress papers are usually made with less surface sizing than offset papers. Besides making the surface uniformly receptive to the letterpress impression, less sizing promotes better opacity and a softer, more flexible book paper. However, the increased surface sizing on offset papers contributes mullen, fold strength, and durability.

Gravure

Gravure is probably the least overall demanding process upon paper; however, it demands the utmost in smoothness and levelness.

Offset or lithographic

Since water (which softens paper) is used in direct contact with the paper in the offset process, paper requirements are radically different than for letterpress or gravure. Some of the reasons offset demands greater surface strength papers include:

- The water (fountain solution) used to keep ink from spreading to the nonimage areas is transferred to the paper, lowering its surface strength.
- The blanket used to transfer the image from the plate to the sheet is tacky and exerts a certain amount of pulling force on the surface of the sheet.
- The ink used in offset is usually much tackier than that used for letterpress, adding to the pulling force upon the surface of the paper.
- The blanket makes complete contact with the sheet, exerting pressure on all parts of the sheet, including the edges. No part is missed in contrast to letterpress where only the image area is in contact with the paper.

Essentially, the offset process softens the sheet and at the same time exerts more and varied pressure upon its surface than other printing processes. In order for paper to perform well in offset printing, these factors have to be taken into consideration and extra strength built into the sheet. Otherwise, the sheet will perform poorly, or not at all.

To meet surface strength demands, offset paper must be highly water-resistant. Paper with inadequate resistance to water softening exhibits such properties as milking, piling, whitening, etc., and thus degrades print quality, increases waste, and slows down production by requiring that the press be shut down periodically to clean the accumulated material from the blanket. Offset sheets must resist picking, fiber lifting, and splitting; also, the paper must be free of bits or flakes of coating or anything loosely adhered to the surface that will be picked off by the blanket. More surface sizing for offset printing results in stiffer or less limp papers than letterpress papers. Anything loose on the paper surface is picked up by the blanket, thus leaving an unprinted spot where it was picked off. It is transferred to the plate and prints as a "hickey" until manually removed.

Scale, calender, and coating may either be picked off the sheet by the blanket whereupon they become water receptive and do not print, or, if not picked off, they are poorly ink receptive.

Since offset printing is a chemical process, the paper, fountain solution, and ink must be chemically compatible. Surface pH of the paper is important. If too acidic, the paper can react with the ink and prevent its setting or drying, resulting in offsetting, blocking, smearing, etc. Offset printing paper must also be free of materials that can get into the fountain solution, changing its composition. If a sharp distinction between printing and non-printing areas is not maintained, scumming and tinting results.

Moisture content of paper is very important and should be in equilibrium with a relative humidity of 45-50% for sheet-fed printing. Ideally, the RH of the paper should be the same as the pressroom air at the time of printing. Moisture imbalance between paper and environment causes problems related to paper dimensional stability. Moisture content is critical for rolls sheeted prior to printing because out-of-equilibrium moisture can cause the same problems as when paper is made for sheet-fed presses. Printing problems such as wrinkling, misregister, doubling, slurring, web breaks, and folder jam-ups have been attributed to moisture or moisture-produced defects.

Offset places relatively little demand upon the smoothness of the sheet in halftone printing as compared to letterpress. In general, the surface smoothness has little effect upon dot structure in offset printing. One of offset's advantages is that the compressible blanket allows the printing of halftone dots on antique stock with nearly the fidelity one could get using paper with a smooth surface. However, in some cases, depending upon the type of roughness and the image being printed, certain harmful effects can be traced to the lack of surface smoothness. Levelness, on the other hand, can be very important in offset. Wild, uneven formations will produce mottled, blotchy solids and tints.

Web offset

In web offset, printing is from a continuous web of paper at high speeds (1000 ft/min and up) with folding or sheeting just before delivery. High speeds necessitate quick drying, and at this point in time, practical technology dictates the use of heat-gas flame, hot air, or a combination of the two: hence, heat-set inks. In flashing off the ink solvents, web temperatures sometimes reach 350° F. The web must then be cooled (chill rolls) down to about room temperature to harden the ink film.

Two types of web offset presses are used. The *blanket-to-blanket perfecting* press prints both sides of from one to six colors in line, dries the web, and folds, sheets, or rewinds the web. Over 80% of the web offset presses are of the blanket-to-blanket perfecting type. The *common impression cylinder* (C.I.C.) press prints one side of the web, sends it through a dryer, prints the second side, and dries again before folding.

Web offset has economic advantages in that the job is completed in less time; it is capable of excellent work on lighter weight papers; paper is less expensive in roll form. Web offset is a more complete and more specialized system than sheet-fed. It is a continuous flow, high-speed process that cannot afford interruptions. As in the papermaking process, any interruption in flow with the ensuing waste results in prohibitive costs. Whereas a paper defect might cause a sheet-fed offset press to waste 50 impressions or less, waste on a web offset press can and often does run into thousands of impressions.

All factors affecting offset printability, in general, except those specifically related to sheeting, apply to web offset. Web offset places additional requirements upon paper:

Tension. High tension (approx. five pounds/linear inch) is required to positively control the web as it travels through the press. Movement, wandering sidewise, jerking, flapping, etc., cannot be tolerated and at the same time maintain print quality, print register, cut-off register, and fold register. Grain direction tension is exerted on the sheet during web offset printing. In sheet-fed printing, the tension or pull is exerted across grain.

Adequate internal bond strength. The web is subjected to strong forces from tacky ink and blankets pulling on opposite sides of the sheet at the same time. If internal bond strength is inadequate, delamination can occur.

Mechanical conditions of the roll. Defects that cause minimal problems in sheet-fed printing can make web printing impossible. Some paper defects that cause web breaks include: bursts, calender cuts, blade cuts, cracked edges, mill pasters, fiber cuts, slime holes, baggy edges, tight edges, slack rolls, poor winding, glue on edge of roll, and wrinkles. A slight grain direction calender cut would stop a sheet-fed press but could possibly travel through a web press.

Moisture. The moisture content of a coated web offset sheet is critical. A high moisture level can lead to blistering, especially with heavy ink coverage on both sides of the sheet. The moisture is sealed into the sheet by the coating and ink layer and vaporized by the high dryer temperatures required in web offset. Essentially, the trapped moisture that is unable to expand, explodes, creating a blister. There must be enough moisture to allow for runnability and to minimize the problems of poor register and mechanical conditions, but not enough to cause blistering problems.

Binding

Common binding methods include edition binding, side stitching, adhesive binding, and saddle-wire binding. Grain direction must parallel the binding edge for proper leafing or turning of the pages and to prevent distortion of the pages at the binding edge.

Edition binding. Edition binding has been the conventional binding method for many years. Four pages of end leaves (usually 80 lb basis weight) are glued to the first and last signatures. The machine-collated signatures (normally in 16 or 32 pages) are sewn together on a special sewing machine which sews signature to signature. The sewn books are squared up and glued in the squared position then trimmed top, front, and foot. The book is rounded on the back (concave front) and joints made by a rolling action on the round-backing machine. A strip of crash cloth and a strip of kraft paper is glued to the backbone in such a manner that the cloth extends outward from each side about an inch. The cloth extension is reinforcing for the *joint* or hinge area of the book. The book is cased in by machine (cover attached) which glues the outer end leaf and joints (front and back) to the inside of the cover and squares the book in the cover. The book is then passed to the pressing section of the machine which applies heat and pressure to set the adhesive. The book is then wrapped, packed, and shipped. Sewn bindings demand paper that is strong enough to resist cutting by the thread, resistant to cracking at the fold, and stiff enough to handle in the sewing operation. For the latter, each signature is placed over the sewing saddle by hand in the hand-fed operation. Also, the squareness and tightness of the sewn book depends on how the paper responds to glue.

Side-stitched binding. Side-stitched or side-sewn books are sewn parallel to the backbone through the entire book much as one who sews two pieces of cloth together with a sewing machine. Paper requirements for side-stitched work are probably all related to handling by prior operations, i.e., folding, collating, etc.

Adhesive binding. In adhesive binding, the pages of the book are bound (glued) together with adhesive: no sewing, wiring, etc. On an adhesive binder, folded and gathered signatures are cut apart into single sheets to get adhesive to each of the inside pages of the signature. The backbone is leveled, roughed, or patterned, and a layer of adhesive is applied over the entire surface. A paper cover may be applied directly on top of the tacky adhesive, completing the book except for trimming; or, stretchcloth or paper may be applied on top of the tacky adhesive and the book is finished as an adhesive casebound book. In this event, the subsequent steps in manufacturing are identical to those of a sewn book.

Principal in paper factors is the ability of the adhesive to get into the paper and form a strong bond. It is common knowledge that papers which are closely knit, hard, smooth, and nonporous are very difficult to bind with adhesive while open, bulky, rough, porous sheets usually bind well and produce exceptionally strong books.

Factors believed to determine the relative adhesive "bindability" of a sheet are smoothness, porosity, receptivity, and caliper. Various test methods are used to measure how easily pages tear out of the finished book. Both the effectiveness of the adhesive and the paper strength are involved. Instruments have been designed to determine the number of times a page can be flexed before it detaches from the backbone of the book and the force required to pull the page from the backbone. The *subway test* determines the damage to a book after its pages have been separated in its middle and the book has been bent completely backward, cover to cover, thereby subjecting the page joints at the backbone to maximum bending strain. The Library Institute has established a Library Book-Testing Laboratory at Rochester Institute of Technology for the evaluation of binding materials.

Saddle-wire binding. Saddle-wire binding used for pamphlets and the like makes use of wire staples through the center of the pamphlet to hold it together. For a seemingly simple operation, paper plays an important part: it has to be strong enough to hold the staples and fold without breaking. Folding requirements on the cover paper are especially tough; it should fold 180° without breaking or cracking. Paper folds more easily and neatly when its direction of fold parallels its grain direction. It becomes more difficult to fold in a direction perpendicular to its grain or cross grain. For this reason, grain direction parallel to the folded edge is preferred.

Trimming

No matter how a book is bound, it must be trimmed. The paper must trim without shattering the edge, breaking out minute chunks of coating, filler, etc.; blocking under trimming pressure; and dulling the trimmer knives.

Moisture

The moisture content of paper bound into books is important. Moisture imbalance causes such defects as wavy edges, wrinkles, starts, and buckles.

Gusseting

In the TAPPI *Glossary of Paper Terms for Web and Sheet-Fed Offset Printing*, gusseting is defined as "a waviness and, in extreme cases, actual creases at the heads of the inner pages of a closed head press signature. Gusseting occurs because the inner pages of a folded, closed head signature cannot move

independently of the adjacent pages to compensate for progressively varying centers and radii of curvature of backbone fold from the outside pages
to the center pages of the signature. As a result, the paper in the center of
the signature is forced forward at the backbone but, being restrained at the
head, it assumes corrugations or waves and, in extreme cases, these waves
fold over and become hard wrinkles.''

Bulk requirements

Papers for book publishing are generally manufactured to bulk rather than
finish. Book cases and packaging carton sizes are often precalculated from
the bulk specification of the paper. It is important that paper conform to
the prescribed bulk specification. For example, a 10% bulk error on a set
of books of 30 in. length could cause three extra inches. Generally, an error
to the thin side is more tolerable than to the thick side. High-bulk paper is
wanted for some books of fewer pages in order to give the book more
substance or to reduce basis weight for a given bulk. Bulk is generally specified
as pages per inch under a pressure of 35 lbs psi to simulate the conditions
of hard binding. Smashed bulk may differ from that calculated from the
thickness of one or more sheets due to the compressibility of a number of
sheets under pressure. A simple calculation to convert four-sheet caliper to
pages per inch and vice versa is done as follows with the factor of eight:

$$1000 \times \frac{8}{4 \text{ sheet caliper}} = \text{pages per inch}$$

$$1000 \times \frac{8}{\text{pages per inch}} = 4 \text{ sheet caliper}$$

One sheet in a book provides two pages, and pages per inch will always
be an even number. The bulk range of paper extends from approximately
310 pages per inch for high bulk to 800 pages per inch for low bulk for a
basis weight of 25 × 38 in. – 50 lb. The relationship of finish or surface
and bulk expressed as pages per inch for various papers is given in Table 11.1.

There are several useful relationships for comparing bulk characteristics
of various book publishing papers and for various basis weights. One relationship is *apparent density* which is obtained by dividing the basis weight
as 25 × 38 in. – 500 by the paper's thickness in points. For example,

Apparent density for:

50 lb – 310 pages per inch is $\dfrac{50}{6.45} = 7.75$ lbs per point thickness

50 lb – 800 pages per inch is $\dfrac{50}{2.5} = 20$ lbs per point thickness

Another relationship is bulking index and is obtained by dividing the single-sheet thickness in thousands by the basis weight, thus:

50 lb – 310 pages per inch is $\dfrac{.00645}{50}$ or .000129 inches thickness per lb

50 lb – 800 pages per inch is $\dfrac{.0025}{50}$ or .0005 inches thickness per lb

A third relationship for comparing bulking characteristics is stated as points of thickness per pound of basis weight as 25 × 38 in. – 500. A point of thickness equals one thousandth of an inch. For example, two papers—one a high bulk and the other a low bulk—have a thickness of 5.5 and 3 points respectively for 25 × 38 in. – 50 lb basis weight. Their bulking characteristics stated in points per pound is:

High bulk paper is: $\dfrac{5.5}{50}$ = 0.110 points per pound

Low bulk paper is: $\dfrac{3.5}{50}$ = .070 points per pound

NASTA specifications

Papers for elementary and high-school textbooks are required to meet NASTA specifications; that is, those as prescribed by the National Association of State Textbook Administrators, formerly known as BMI. NASTA specifications require a minimum bursting strength, tear, and opacity for given weight ranges as well as a maximum permissible gloss. A tolerance of 1/16 in. ± the prescribed bulk is permitted. NASTA specifications also state that a minimum allowable basis weight be used, depending upon the grade-school level of the textbook. Uncoated textbook papers must be free from groundwood or unbleached chemical pulp. Machine and film-coated groundwood papers may be used in the manufacture of textbooks, providing they meet all NASTA specifications and have a specified minimum brightness. NASTA specifications for end-leaf paper include a prescribed basis weight and a minimum value for bursting strength and fold.

While NASTA specifications were originated and intended only for El-Hi textbooks, they may occasionally be prescribed for other applications such as college textbooks.

Permanency considerations

Permanency of the paper is sometimes a consideration. Papers whose life will be short or temporary are suitable for paperbacks, children's books, and workbooks. Papers for textbooks, bibles, and reference books are generally required to have a longer life expectancy. Library editions may require a long-life type of paper.

Availability

Book publishing papers are generally not stocked as are commercial printing papers. Since book publishing papers are made to specific bulks, shades, and sheet or roll sizes, they are usually available on a making order basis. Sizes ordered are related in some multiple to the book page size.

Papers for books by type and application

Trade books

Papers for trade books are usually bulky and are often made in off-white or cream-white shades. Tradebooks such as biographies, memoirs, and lengthy novels may require lower bulk papers. Laid finish papers may occasionally be used. Trade books are generally printed in one-color for type and line illustration.

Textbooks

Papers for textbooks are generally manufactured in a blue-white shade for good halftone contrast and for single and multicolor printing. College level textbooks are generally printed one color whereas El-Hi textbooks are printed one-, two- and four-color. The trend has been to multicolor printing with more illustrations and pictorial subjects for textbooks. Matte-finish coated papers are often used to give better quality halftone and color illustrations. NASTA specifications are required for El-Hi textbook papers but not for college textbooks except at the option of the purchaser. The common basis weights are 25 $\times$ 38 in. – 45, 50, 55, and 60 lb per ream. College textbooks are manufactured in relatively limited quantities per edition whereas El-Hi textbooks are manufactured in much larger quantities per edition.

Workbook, drawing, and coloring books

Papers for workbooks, drawing, and coloring books are generally required to have only a temporary life. Consequently, papers for these applications may often contain mechanical pulps. They generally have a toothy surface and are hardsized for crayon and water coloring. Printing is usually confined to one color with light coverage.

Reference books

Papers used for reference books vary in type and basis weight, depending upon bulk requirements and the nature of the book. Matte-coated papers may be used for multicolor illustrations. The weight range extends from 25 $\times$ 38 in. – 20 to 60 lb per ream.

Lightweight printing papers

Historically, lightweight printing papers have been selected for a limited number of book uses such as Bibles, dictionaries, and handbooks. The two major reasons for using the lightweight papers are bulk reduction and weight reduction.

While many books can be used to illustrate the needs for lightweight papers, the Bible is the one book which has the closest relationship to the specialized craft of lightweight paper manufacturing. The Bible contains as many as 1800 pages, depending on the amount of additional material, such as maps and concordances. In order to produce a portable book, the paper should have a bulk range of 1000 pages per inch to 1800 pages per inch. This bulk range of 30 to 17 lb, 25 × 38 in. – 500. Before the 1960s, most Bibles were printed by sheet-fed letterpress. During the 1960s, web offset developed into the by sheet-fed letterpress. During the 1960s, web offset developed into the primary process for Bible printing. Paper requirements changed as more lightweight paper was made for offset, and several mills developed strong-sized offset Bible paper with the high-quality appearance of letterpress grades. The staining and gilding of Bibles changed as the paper changed, and a fundamental production problem was resolved. This problem involved the maintenance of Bible signatures left after the completion of a run. The high cost of printing and paper under the sheet-fed letterpress process required that an inventory of odd signatures be kept for the following printing. With the change to offset printing came the elimination of this large inventory of signatures.

The changes that occurred within the Bible industry also affected the reference book and trade book fields. The prominence of sheet-fed and web offset led to a new family of lightweight papers. Mills that were not prepared to change from the manufacture of lightweight sheet-fed letterpress paper to lightweight offset paper eliminated themselves from this business, while other mills entered the field with strong, bright, opaque lightweight paper manufactured on modern high-speed papermaking equipment, increasing the capacity and output of lightweight printing paper. This increased capacity matched the increased demand for lighter weight paper; for while lightweight paper consumption for religious books doubled in the decade from 1960 to 1970, the consumption of lightweight paper for reference books such as dictionaries, encyclopedias, handbooks, manuals, directories, scientific, and professional books increased five-fold in the same period. The great information explosion has been swelling text matter and increasing distribution costs, thus necessitating a move toward lighter, less bulky paper.

Specialized Bible paper should be considered as a book paper that requires a certain amount of craftmanship on the part of the printer and binder. It also requires care on the part of the papermaker. Press performance is affected greatly by defects in lightweight paper such as curl, baggy rolls, and wavy edges. Static, which may be present in both heavy and light papers, will hinder smooth press performance in lightweight paper. The papermaker must make lightweight paper with uniformity across the web and throughout the run to prevent an uneven caliper profile, moisture imbalance, weight variation, and opacity variation.

The printer, in turn, must become tolerant toward the handling of lightweight paper, and he must be prepared to make the necessary adjustments to overcome minor paper defects. Paper should be conditioned according to proper conditioning procedures, and covered after skids, rolls, and cartons are opened.

Care should be exercised in feeding sheet-fed paper by reducing the air blast and vacuum to compensate for the reduced paper weight. Feed rollers should be adjusted to prevent overdriving the paper on the feed board. On offset presses, ink tack should be reduced and impression pressure should be increased to produce best printed results. To prevent curling, fountain water should be kept as low as possible. For best letterpress reproduction, a kiss impression is necessary, more so with lightweight paper because there is little paper bulk to absorb the impression. To improve delivery, wedges should be used to help the paper jog properly. Auxiliary equipment, such as mechanical static eliminators and sprays, usually help to structure an even pile of delivered paper. On web presses, web tension should be maintained uniformly across the web, and oven temperature should be kept as low as possible.

In the bindery, proper care must be taken with folding equipment to prevent erratic feeding and wrinkling. One of the great advantages of lightweight paper is its ability to be folded into 64-page signatures. A problem develops when air is trapped within the signature and produces gussets. Gussets may be controlled by proper use of perforations to enable air and paper to move enough to remove the gusset-forming wrinkles.

Lightweight papers can be improved by increasing ink holdout and decreasing moisture penetration through the use of better sizing material. Strength and uniformity should be a goal in lightweight papermaking to improve runnability on any press. Great care should be spent in the finishing areas to prevent poorly slit or poorly trimmed paper from reaching the printer. Above all, quality control in a lightweight paper mill must be maintained at a high level.

Special interest books

Paper for special interest books varies considerably in type, depending upon the purpose they must fulfill. An art book, for example, may be printed on a glossy enamel paper for maximum fidelity of reproduction. A cookbook may require a water-resistant surface.

End-leaf applications

An end-leaf paper must have high tear and folding strength. It must accept moisture from the gluing down to the cover and dry without distortions such as welting or waving. As the end-leaf paper releases moisture during and after binding, it should not distort the contacting pages of the book. White and colored end-leaf papers are used; basis weights range from 60 to 100 lb for 25 × 38 in. ream, with 80 lb as the most commonly used weight. End-leaf papers may or may not be printed.

Book jackets and cover applications

Papers used as a book jacket or a cover must meet the requirements of physical stamina and handling as well as providing high printing contrast. The cover, or book jacket, often plays an important part in persuading one to select the book. Papers for these applications may also be varnished or lacquered for aesthetic enhancement and to prevent soiling. Coated one side papers are commonly used, and the weight range may extend from 25 × 38 in. – 60 lb per ream to a 10 pt coated one side bristol or cover.

Trends in book publishing

Press and bindery runs for books are getting shorter. The trend is to lower the edition quantity, lowering the risk of the title not selling and reducing warehousing and inventory cost while requiring immediate reprints to keep the title in stock. Book ordering quantities will become smaller.

Turnaround time for producing a book from manuscript has been considerably shortened in the last few years and there is constant pressure for still shorter production times. Shorter lead times are required lest the subject of the book be outdated or lose the public's interest before it is published. This entails tight scheduling, not only for production through the various stages of building a book, but shorter delivery times for raw materials used in book production.

Building a book more economically includes such things as more efficient equipment, reduced paper waste, better trained operating personnel, more reliable raw materials with which to work, and changes in publishers' thinking regarding the basic purpose of a book versus the designer's whims. The trend continues to a complete book manufacturing facility under one roof and to streamlining book production systems. Some noted changes in this area include:

- Generally faster, more efficient and reliable equipment; reduced make-ready time and waste with increased productivity of presses and binding equipment.

- Increased use of web offset for more classes of books, including shorter run editions, and a decline of sheet-fed offset for book printing.

- Use of lighter weight papers through web offset printing.

- Use of more fully coated matte papers and pigmented surface coated papers in place of uncoated paper for better quality four-color printing and reduction of glare and for adding more bulk proportionate to the weight as compared to glossy supercalendered papers.

- Use of cheaper synthetic materials for casebound covers.

- Use of more in-line equipment, such as the Cameron Book Production System and automated binding lines.

- Less tipping-in of illustrations printed on coated papers; more utilization of papers capable of combination line and illustration reproduction.

- The trend to paperbacks for quality work and some textbooks.

- More adhesive binding (paperback and casebound); less of the more expensive sewn books.

- Some trend, at least a beginning, to product standardization as to trim size, number of pages (in multiples of press forms) and paper stock (perhaps a choice of three or four standard sheets).

Along with the trend to lower basis weight is the endless desire for more opacity. The trend to bluer-white papers also continues.

As to printing equipment, there is a difference of opinion as to size trends. One group believes the trend is to larger sheet-fed and wider web presses. Another group believes that the trend is to smaller sheet-fed and narrower webs. The latter base their opinion upon the need for fast makeready and fast, efficient machines for short-run work. There will be more in-line systems of book printing like the Cameron Belt Press for the printing of Bibles, encyclopedias, and directories and possibly having the capability of printing halftones and in multicolor.

Another nebulous area is the trend to more two and four-color illustrations. While this has undoubtedly been true in the past, there is the possibility that economic or money-saving steps may slow or reverse this trend, except for specialized, high-class work.

Major trends in our society which are influencing the book publishing industry include more people are receiving more education; education has become a continuing, life-long pursuit; and multi-media educational means are used in the classroom, that is, the textbook is no longer the sole means for instruction.

Future developments in knowledge dissemination which may affect traditional methods in the book publishing industry are micro-publishing either as miniaturized images on film or paper for later enlargement to the original size, cathode-ray tube display devices, the concept of on-demand printing of books by electrostatic or electronic methods and systems for piping-in information from libraries or information storage centers to the user or reader. Adaptation of electrostatic printing technology to the Cameron Belt Press principle may make it possible to use computer-controlled composition and to change composition instantly and without the need to stop and replate the press for a new title.

Table 11.1. Relationship of finish and bulk for various papers

Finish or Surface	Bulk Range in Pages Per Inch for 25 x 38 - 50 lb Basis Weight
Antique high bulk uncoated	310-380
Antique uncoated	390-460
Eggshell finish uncoated	470-560
M. F. or E. F. finish uncoated	570-670
Matte finish coated	600-700
Plate or supercalendered uncoated	700-800
Plate finish or supercalendered coated	760-820

Glossary

Adhesive binding   The fastening of loose leaves into a bound book by the application of a hot-melt adhesive to their binding surface.

Apparent density   The ratio of a paper's basis weight to its thickness. Expressed as pounds per point of thickness.

Backing   The operation of flaring out the rounded back of a book to insure it will remain permanently rounded and to provide the joint at which the cover will hinge and the pages will bend when turned. Also serves to lock the book to its cover.

Backbone   See "Spine."

Book bulk   The overall thickness of a given number of sheets in a book.

Book jacket   A separate printed paper or clear plastic wrapping which fits loosely around the cover of a book. Original purpose was to prevent soiling and abrasion of the cover. Now used mainly to attract the buyer's attention and to identify the book.

Buckled pages   A distortion of the pages next to the backbone of a book. Caused by the gathering and binding of signatures which have a very low moisture content and which subsequently absorb moisture and grow sufficiently in the grain direction to produce buckling.

Bulk   The measured thickness of a pile of sheets under a specified pressure simulating that used in manufacturing hardbound books. Expressed as the bulking number or the number of pages required to bulk one inch (PPI).

Bulking index   The number obtained by dividing the caliper of a single thickness of a given paper by its basis weight. May be expressed decimally as inches of thickness per pound.

Bulking thickness   The average thickness of a single sheet as determined from a stack of sheets or its bulking number. Bulking thickness will generally be less than the measured caliper of a single thickness due to the compressibility of a stack of sheets under pressure.

Caliper   The measured thickness of a single sheet by the use of a micrometer when a specified static load is applied for a minimum specified time.

Casing in   The assembly of a book into its final form by inserting it into its cover, lining up, pasting down the end sheets, and clamping the cased-in book under pressure for a period of time to maintain its shape as the adhesive dries.

Collating   The assembly of individual leaves for loose-leaf, mechanical, or manifold binding.

Edge stain   Application of color or dye to one or more edges of a book to overcome a soiled appearance due to handling.

Edition binding   The mass binding of identical books by the use of automatic machinery.

End paper   A heavy weight, strong paper attached to the front and back signatures of a book and which is pasted to the inside of the front and back covers of a casebound book. Serves to hold the hard cover and book together. All end paper for El-Hi books must meet NASTA specifications for basis weight, burst, and fold. Also called end sheet, end leaf, or lining.

Format   The type size, style, margins, layout, and other printing specifications for the production of a book.

Gathering   The assembly of printed signatures or book sections in their proper arrangement for binding.

Gilding   The application of gold leaf to the edges of a book for decoration.

Gusseting   A waviness or actual creases created at the heads of the inner pages during the folding of closed head-press signatures.

Gutter   The inside margins between the facing pages of a book.

Hardbound book   A book bound in a hard cover or case consisting of binder board covered with cloth or some other material.

Headbands   Strips of colored cloth which are adhered to the spine and which protrude slightly at the bottom and top of the book. They provide decoration and protection to the spine as a book is pulled off the shelf.

Hinge   A depression between the cover and spine of a hardbound book which acts as a hinge for opening the cover.

Imposition   The arrangement of printed images on a press sheet and its positioning into the press in accordance with a plan to produce signatures whose pages are in the proper numbered sequence.

Library binding   A strong binding for withstanding the use to which library books are subjected.

Lining-up   The gluing of a strip of fabric covered by a strip of lining paper to the back of a book preparatory to its casing in.

NASTA   The National Association of State Textbook Administrators, an organization which develops manufacturing standards and specifications for textbooks as well as for the various materials used in their construction and known as NASTA specifications. Formerly BMI specifications.

Page flex test Measurement of the number of times the page of a book may be flexed back and forth through a specified arc and with a selected tensile force applied at its bound edge. The number of flexes required to pull the page out of its binding is taken as the measurement.

Page pull test The tensile force per linear inch of binding edge required to pull a page out of its binding under specified conditions.

Paperback A book whose cover consists of paper trimmed flush with the body of the book in contrast to a hard cover. Also called soft cover.

Points of thickness The thickness of a single sheet of paper expressed in points where each point denotes one thousandth of an inch.

Roughing Mechanical roughing of the backbone for greater surface area and penetration of adhesive binding into the edge fibers of the sheets. Produces a stronger adhesive binding.

Rounding The shaping of the backbone of the book into a rounded, convex contour. Rounding produces a concave shape to the opposite or fore edge and prevents it from protruding beyond the cover in time and with usage.

Saddle stitching The binding of individual or inserted signatures by placing wire staples through their centerfolds.

Side sewing Binding a book by sewing through the side of its bound edge within a short distance from its back edge. Produces a strongly bound book which does not open completely flat. Sometimes called McCain sewing.

Side wire stitching Binding a book by fastening the side of its bound edge with wire staples.

Signature A section of a book and a unit of binding. Consists of a printed two-side sheet which when folded produces a group of pages arranged in numerical sequence.

Smashing A mechanical compression of the bound signatures of a book to reduce swelling and eliminate air for a more compact binding.

Smyth sewn Binding of signatures by sewing through their centerfolds and to each other. Produces a strongly bound book that is easily opened.

Softbound   See "Paperback."

Spine   The bound edge or backbone of a book whose purpose is to keep the book straight and upright and maintain its shape.

Starts   The development of uneven edges of a trimmed book due to a varying growth or shrinkage of individual signatures from moisture adjustment which occurs after gathering, binding, and trimming.

Subway test   A subjective test simulating the stresses of distortion applied to a paperback by a subway reader. The paperback is bent through 360° to bring its covers back to back so it may be held in one hand.

Bibliography

Book Production Industry. Market Publications, Inc., New Canaan, CT, (bi-monthly publication).

Benevento, F.S. *The Offset Press*. Audiovisual. Graphic Arts Technical Foundation, Pittsburgh, 1970.

Bruno, M.H., ed. *Glossary of Paper Terms for Web and Sheet-Fed Offset Printing*. Technical Association of the Pulp and Paper Industry, Atlanta, 1971.

Bureau, W.H. *What the Printer Should Know About Paper*. Graphic Arts Technical Foundation, Pittsburgh, 1982.

Casey, J.P. *Pulp and Paper*. Vol. 3, forthcoming. Interscience, New York.

Hartsuch, P.J. *Chemistry for the Graphic Arts*. Graphic Arts Technical Foundation, Pittsburgh, 1979.

Lee, M. *Bookmaking*. R.R. Bowker, New York, 1979.

The Lithographers Manual. Graphic Arts Technical Foundation, Pittsburgh, 1980.

Manufacturing Standards and Specifications for Textbooks of the National Association of State Textbook Administrators. The Book Manufacturers Institute. Ridgefield, CT, 1982.

Strauss, V. *The Printing Industry*. Printing Industries of America, Arlington, VA, 1967.

Section VII
Business and Writing Papers

Charles T. Ray, Editor

12
Safety Papers

Robert H. Mosher

Introduction

Classification

The major classification within the *safety papers* product area are grades used to produce checks and other legal forms and documents treated to make visible any attempts to alter the writing or printing on their surface. They can be produced by the addition of certain chemicals into the beater or headbox when the paper is being made, by a surface sizing treatment or coating, or by printing or embossing an overall design onto the surface utilizing alteration-sensitive inks. Techniques for introducing the special compounds into the beater or on the machine are only of significance to the papermaker, but the converting industry is also involved with the various coating, saturating, and printing techniques. *Anti-counterfeit papers* are a special category of safety papers which have been manufactured or treated so their identity can be verified by visual or chemical means. Another category includes *safe papers* which can be easily and completely destroyed in order to protect the information on their surfaces.

Basic principles

The principle upon which most safety papers are based is the ability to exhibit telltale reactions when the surface is altered. Certain inks or coatings used change color when contacted by acids, alkalis, or bleaching agents: some blur and diffuse the coating or printing over the area in contact with the altering material, while the other treatments result in the bleeding of a water- or oil-soluble dyestuff when attempts are made to remove or alter a print, stamp, or seal. The basic protective concepts are similar whether an overall clear or colored saturant or coating or an overall printed design is used.

By using an ink or coating, the color of which is a function of the acid concentration or pH level, any employment of acidic bleaching agents or alkaline compounds can be readily detected by the resulting variations in the color shade in the design or surface appearance. Inks can be made acid-sensitive by the addition of such chemicals as zinc chloride, hexamethyl and pentamethyl monoethyl-p-rosaniline, diazo dye from tetrazotized o-toluidine, sodium naphthenate, sodium hydroxide, or monosodium phosphate. Treating compounds which contain metallic salts of fatty acids usually change shade when treated with a detergent. Aniline hydrochloride discolors by the decomposition of the hydrochloride when a bleaching agent is brought into contact with the paper. Many common dyestuffs change color or even become colorless with change in pH.

Colorless or slightly colored manganous compounds which are changed to color manganic compounds by oxidation have been suggested as protective wash coatings. Dioxy- and trioxy-benzoic acids and their derivatives produce color reactions with even weak oxidizing agents; these are almost impossible to reverse or bleach out even by subsequent application of the most powerful reducing agents. The use of a colorless pyrogallol wash coating which turns brown with the introduction of an oxidizing type bleaching agent has been suggested. A paper containing polyoxybenzoic acid does not react with acids, but does provide an almost complete protection against partial chemical falsification or erasure because of a color change. A special preparation has been produced which is sensitive to oxidizing agents and the resulting stain cannot be eliminated by reducing agents (*1, 2*). The sheet can be treated with a wash coating of ferric salts such as ferric acetate, followed by a suitable acid-soluble ferrocyanide such as lead ferrocyanide. The final solution used is a mixture of equal parts of pyrogallol carboxylic acid and pentagalloyl glucose which has been brought up to a pH level of 3.0 to 3.5 by the addition of a suitable alkali.

A new technique involves the use of another class of reducible inorganic salts reportedly resistant to decomposition by oxidizing agents. The salts used are selected from a group consisting of manganous tellurite, barium tellurite, and alkali selenite.

Types of safety papers

To guard against the sending of secret messages by prisoners or other suspect persons who might be writing with invisible or sympathetic inks, papers have been produced that immediately develop any writing on their surface using invisible inks into visible characters without the subsequent application of heat or chemical reagents. The sensitive-coated paper first utilized in these applications consisted of a paper base coated with a clay-based compound containing a mechanically incorporated dyestuff which reacted when moistened or when written upon with an acidic invisible ink to produce a highly visible green color. This particular sheet did not react, however, with alkaline-based invisible inks to produce distinctly visible writing; a second ingredient was subsequently incorporated into the paper coating. This ingredient reacted with alkaline-type sympathetic or invisible inks to produce a visible red coloration. The paper, called "Sensicoat," immediately exposed the writing from either acidic or neutral invisible inks in the green color while with alkaline invisible inks the writing appeared in red. Thus, all markings made on the paper were clearly visible to the censors or other authorities. In evaluating the permanence of these self-developing colors, tests have shown that they will last for months. The advantage of this sheet lies in the fact that the prisoners or suspect persons may be permitted to write freely upon the specially-prepared paper with any of the standard visible inks.

The paper, as originally developed, was a 23-lb specially coated sheet, basis 17 × 22 in.–500 ream size, with the color sensitizer incorporated into the coating. Its high cost and relatively low weight were factors leading to the subsequent development of a lighter, uncoated, and much less expensive sheet.

The improved paper specified an uncoated stock, very sensitive to writing with all types of solutions which could be used as sympathetic inks, as unreactive as possible to humidity and ordinary handling, and low in cost. A series of laboratory and plant experiments resulted in a paper which could be manufactured in one plant including the incorporation of the special dyes required in the sensitizing formula. The new paper was called "Anilith."

Safe papers

Another interesting grade identified as *safe paper* is required for the transmission of government codes, military orders, and other documents which must be preserved in secrecy and must be completely destroyed in an emergency to prevent their falling into alien or unfriendly hands. Most of these papers will burn and leave practically no residual ash, but in many cases this is not a sufficiently fast and reliable procedure for destruction. Telltale smoke may linger, and unless the ash has been completely decomposed, it may be possible to reconstruct the contents by means of widely-available scientific detection techniques.

A specially coated paper can be produced which is virtually self-destructing when dipped or submerged in plain water (3). The paper and coating are constructed so that the water permeates throughout the sheet almost instantly and causes a chemical reaction in which gas is instantly developed. The gas loosens and separates the coating from the paper while the bubbles developed within the material of the coating destroy it. Any messages printed or written on the coating are obliterated. A waterleaf-type base paper is recommended that may be surface-sized with starch if required. A suggested reactive coating for the printing side of the paper is shown on the following page.

Component	Parts
Methyl cellulose	6.5
Calcium carbonate	0.8
Water	Sufficient to make a coatable composition

This coating can be applied by the usual aqueous coating procedures and will be quickly decomposed at a high hydrogen ion concentration. Small amounts of plasticizer may be added for additional flexibility, but is not necessary for good results. Instead of methyl cellulose, alternate binders such as gum arabic, dextrine, synthetic water, soluble resins, or glue can be used.

When the application of the face coating has been completed, a second coating is applied to the back side of the sheet. This coating should be applied at a very high viscosity to prevent its penetration into the sheet; it is composed of methyl cellulose or similar binder and an acid such as tartaric, citric, maleic, or lactic. Plasticizers can be added if required. The acid is dissolved in water-free solvent such as anhydrous alcohol so a reaction will not occur during the coating operation.

Anti-counterfeit papers

Anti-counterfeit papers are produced as easily identifiable types similar to the currency or bank note papers which have traditionally utilized the presence of red and blue synthetic or silk fibers incorporated into the sheet during its manufacture on the paper machine (4). The colored fibers are readily visible to the naked eye because they differ both in size and appearance from the cellulosic fiber furnish from which the paper is fabricated. *Identifiable papers* have also been produced where the mark of identification involves added fibers that fluoresce when exposed to ultraviolet light. In the printing of World War II ration books, military identification cards, and various tax and premium stamps, fluorescent cellulosic fibers were incorporated into the paper structure to discourage counterfeiting activity.

In order to increase the effectiveness and reduce the cost of anti-counterfeit papers, the Technical Division of the Government Printing Office has conducted extensive research programs to develop additional types of identifiable papers which would easily distinguish genuine from counterfeit stamps, cards, or tickets by means other than the use of fluorescent fibers.

It was found that ferric chloride-treated fibers incorporated into the structure of the paper to the extent of 0.5% would remain colorless and invisible in the sheet until treated with certain chemical reagents such as potassium ferrocyanide and orthophosphoric acid. Upon treatment they would become visible and individually identifiable by acquiring a distinctive and permanent blue color. These fibers presented several advantages not obtainable with the colored silk or synthetic fibers: they are invisible within the paper structure and therefore remain unknown to counterfeiters, and they are basically identical in composition and appearance with the untreated fibers of the entire sheet of paper. Sheets containing chemically-treated fibers can be tested in the field without requiring the expensive and complex ultraviolet light equipment needed to identify the fluorescent fibers. Once the fibers have been chemically reacted for identification purposes, however, the colors developed are generally irreversible. These fibers are "one use items," while the fluorescent fiber containing sheets may be reused and reidentified any number of times. Unlike fluorescent fibers, the chemically-treated fibers do not lose their effectiveness upon exposure to sunlight, bleaching agents, acids, alkalis, water, oil, or gasoline and, therefore, remain in the paper structure as a permanent means of identification.

As a result of the passage of the Soldier Ballot Bill by Congress, soldiers in the field needed voting forms that could be readily and positively identified by election officials as genuine. The identifying characteristics of this paper had to be incorporated very quickly and with existing papermaking and converting equipment. The paper was expected to withstand the action of salt water, heat, and high humidity without complicated tests to reveal their presence. Several grade designs were submitted to the Armed Forces, and the sheet that eventually received approval consisted of printing a design on both sides of the ballot using an ink invisible under daylight or artificial light but which fluoresced brightly when stimulated by ultraviolet radiation. The fluorescing design was composed of the phrase "Official Federal War Ballot" horizontally repeated and separated by a star between each repetition.

Anti-counterfeit papers can be made by the use of these rather complex identifiable printing or coating techniques, but a commonly seen product can also be manufactured by cylinder machine forming or laminating together a number of plies of colored paper so that when a label, document, or ticket is torn in half, the specific arrangement of the colored layers identifies its authenticity at that time.

Literature cited

1. V. Bausch and A. Schroth, U. S. patent 1,864,116; "Production of Paper for Security Purposes" (1912).
2. V. Bausch and A. Schroth, U. S. patent 2,112,756; "Manufacture of Safety Paper" (1938).
3. C. P. Foote and C. D. Guertin, U. S. patent 2,402,542; "Coated Paper and Method of Making Same" (1946).
4. M. S. Kantrowitz, "New World War Papers and Their Uses," *American Paper Convertor,* 22, 11, 12, 34 (1948).

13
Stamp Papers

Robert M. Williams

Introduction

In the United States, the adhesive postage stamps sold by the U. S. Postal Service are printed at the Bureau of Engraving and Printing in Washington, D.C. The Bureau purchases four kinds of paper for printing postage stamps. The base stock of each of these papers is 100% bleached chemical wood. Since the basis weights are similar, the physical characteristics are comparable. The differences among these papers arise from different press and adhesive requirements. Separate specifications are issued by the Bureau for each of these four papers.

Until recently, most United States postage stamps have been printed in a single color by the intaglio process on web presses that have the facility for applying dextrin adhesive (gum) to the web after the stamps have been printed. This printing process requires purchase of paper in rolls 18.5 in. or more in width (Table 13.1).

Potential bidders are provided with additional information on properties descriptive of paper which has performed satisfactorily in the past. These have been termed *indicative physical requirements* and are not considered restrictive (Table 13.2). The requirements do not include coated paper. The paper must be uniform in thickness, density, and surface characteristics, and must contain a uniform distribution of moisture. The paper must be machine finished, and the degree of sizing should make the paper suitable for the intended use.

While paper is purchased for printing postage stamps by the dry intaglio process, the printing characteristics of the paper are paramount. In the intaglio process, ink is applied to a plate having lines incised in its surface. After the removal of excess ink from the nonprinting areas of the plate surface, ink from the incised engraved lines is transferred to the paper by applying pressure. Formerly, the paper was wet with water before printing so that it might easily be deformed and pick the ink out of the engraving. In the

Table 13.1 Technical requirements for postage stamp papers

Type of paper	Ungummed	Pregummed	Dry gummed	Rotogravure
Type of press	Web intaglio	Intaglio (Offset also)	Web intaglio	Web gravure
Type of stamp	All	Multicolor	Book stamps	
Paper fiber	Bleached Chemical wood	Bleached Chemical wood	Bleached Chemical wood	Bleached Chemical wood
Adhesive	None	Dextrin	Special	Dextrin
Tensile strength, (Kg)				
Machine direction (Min)	6.0	6.0	6.0	6.0
Cross direction (Min)	3.0	4.0	4.0	4.0
Bursting strength, points (Min)	24.0*	25.0	25.0	24.0
Basis weight; grams/sq.m.				
Minimum	82.0	84.0	82.0	83.0
Maximum	90.0	93.0	91.0	95.0
Thickness, mils				
Minimum	3.7	4.7	4.8	4.5
Maximum	4.2	5.3	5.2	5.1
Ash, percent (Max)	11.0	11.0	11.0	12.0
Tensile strength after folding 5 times, Kg.				
Machine direction (Min)	—	3.0	—	—
Cross direction (Min)	—	3.0	—	—
Tear resistance, both directions, grams				
Minimum	40.0	—	—	60.0
Maximum	90.0	—	—	80.0
Opacity (percent)	87.0	—	—	—
pH	4.8	—	—	—
Smoothness, Bekk Seconds				
Minimum	40**	80***	40***	80***
Maximum	100**	160***	160***	—
Form of delivery	Rolls	Sheets	Rolls	Rolls

* Indicative only
** Indicative only; wire side
*** Printing side

modern "dry" process, a minimum of moisture is applied to the paper, and proper transfer of ink is accomplished only when the paper has the proper density and surface characteristics and the press has appropriate means of applying pressure. After the ink is transferred to the paper, the ink is in relief, giving the print a three-dimensional appearance and maximum difficulty for making a counterfeit reproduction. The Bureau of Engraving and Printing has six single-color presses which utilize paper of this type and one larger press that prints in up to nine colors on a web, either 18.5 or 21 in. in width. The single-color presses are utilized for printing food coupons on the same ungummed paper as is used for printing postage stamps.

Fig. 19.12 Ridges in rolls. (courtesy of Mead Corporation)

inks, large solid areas, and spot and overall varnish are examples of the great demands when using coated paper. Naturally the demands will generate a higher incidence of troubles in the printing plant. Since the coating is dead weight and all the strength resides in the basesheet, problems in durability, handling, and cracking at the fold may be encountered. The coating layer is more dense than fiber, so at any given basis weight the coated sheet will be lower in caliper than uncoated paper and therefore lower in stiffness, which will often hurt runnability. The coated surface (calendered or cast) is much smoother than the uncoated and will make closer, more intimate contact with the blanket or plate. This makes for better printability but also can result in greater distortion, curl, trailing edge picking, jam-ups, and similar runnability problems.

In actual practice, uncoated paper is more productive than coated in sheet-fed multicolor printing, but not in web printing. Even in lightweight coated sheets under 40 lb basis, runnability will be better with fewer web breaks and less lint and film build-up on the press with coated paper. Perhaps the strength and uniformity needed for the great number of operations required to make coated paper carries over onto the printing press.

Coated papers can be divided into four groups, depending on the optical characteristic and gloss of the coated surface.

Cast-coated papers. These papers are made by a limited number of manu-

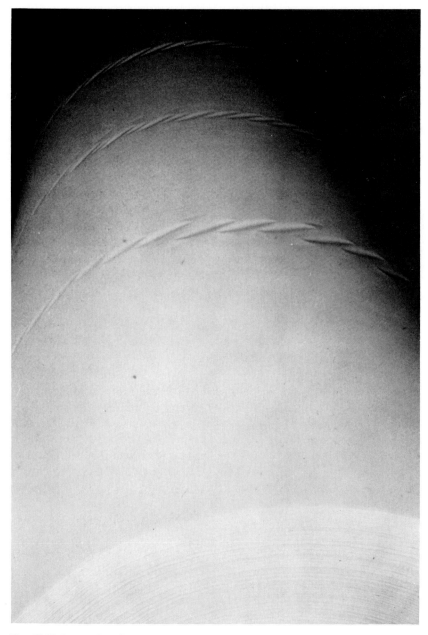

Fig. 19.13 Corrugations (backbones) (ropes). (courtesy of Mead Corporation)

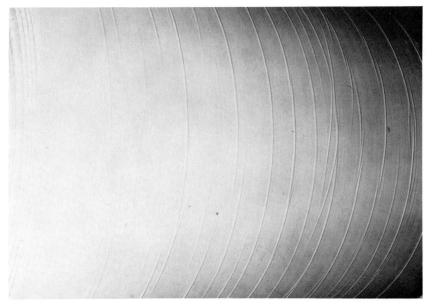

Fig. 19.14 Moisture welts. (courtesy of Mead Corporation)

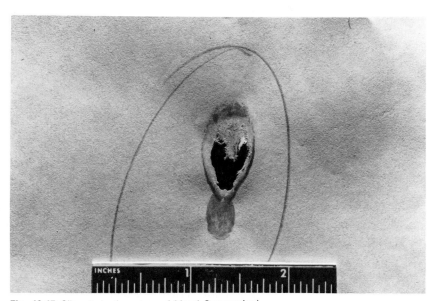

Fig. 19.15 Slime hole. (courtesy of Mead Corporation)

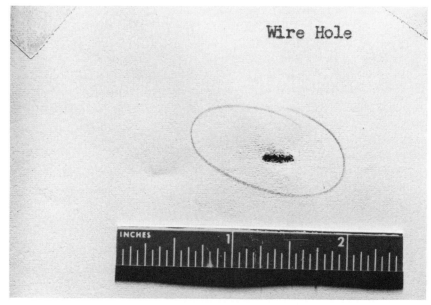

Fig. 19.16 Wire hole. (courtesy of Mead Corporation)

facturers. The wet coated surface is pressed (cast) against a highly polished, chrome-plated drum and dried in place. The papers have the highest gloss, the smoothest surface, and print best by any process. Gloss is usually above 80 when measured on a 75° gloss meter.

Though extremely smooth, cast-coated papers do not experience blanket and plate release problems. The sheet is not calendered and therefore has excellent bulk and stiffness for its weight. Also a high percentage of this grade is made in heavy weights for cover stock and packaging. Both of these factors make for good runnability.

Glossy-coated papers. All papers that have a gloss between 50 and 80. This finish is always obtained by supercalendering or other treatment after coating. In addition to gloss development, this calendering lowers brightness and opacity which must be compensated for in coating and base stock formulation. The same sheet densification which produces the high gloss reduces the caliper, which results in lower stiffness and tearing strength. This can often have major effects on runnability. The gloss development and sheet densification produce excellent ink holdout, snap, and brilliance of the printed image.

Matte-coated papers. Coated papers with a gloss ranging from 7 to 20. These papers normally produce a printed result somewhere between the dull coated and uncoated papers. The printed ink gloss is usually lower than the printed gloss of dull-coated papers. In addition, matte-coated papers are more likely to show a printed mottle (Fig. 19.17). Matte papers print very well with respect to reproduction of detail by offset and sheet-fed gravure. However, the printing of fine detail by letterpress and web gravure printing of any variety is usually not possible even if very high printing pressures are used. They are simply lacking in the necessary smoothness. Since matte-coated papers are calendered very lightly or not at all, they have high bulk and excellent operating stiffness both for sheet and web printing. The porous, unconsolidated surface permits ink to dry very quickly and makes the sheet almost completely resistant to blistering on heat-set offset presses. The same surface, however, makes the dried ink film prone to scuffing and smudge. Since the sheet rarely blisters, the web offset printer may unknowingly overdry it to the point of brittleness and encounter severe cracking at the fold. Its high bulk and unconsolidated surface also can aggravate the cracking.

The use of gloss inks has increased tremendously in recent years. These inks are characterized by somewhat higher tack than normal inks and are often used in large solid areas for dramatic design effects. Both these factors require higher surface strength in the paper and can contribute to blanket release problems, distortion and curl. In the retention of ink holdout, coated papers are superior to uncoated papers. Freedom from mottle, pinpoint smoothness, and paper surface gloss help distinquish between coated papers. Overall, the superior gloss and ink holdout of coated sheets over their

Fig. 19.17 Severe printed mottle. (courtesy of Mead Corporation)

uncoated counterparts will give a pleasing, striking appearance to the finished job due to surface characteristics alone.

Dull-coated papers. These papers have a gloss range from 20 to 50. The snap and brilliance of printed images on dull-coated papers are somewhat less than those printed on glossy-coated papers due to the reduced gloss levels of both paper and ink. These papers are very similar to the glossy papers in the reproduction of detail by offset and by sheet gravure. They may suffer somewhat in reproduction of detail when printed by letterpress and web gravure because of a lack of smoothness.

Due to widely varying methods of manufacture among different paper-makers, dull-coated papers may show great divergence in printability and runnability. In some cases, nonglossing pigments are used in the coating formulation; in others, a high content of nonglossing adhesive may be used as a binder. Both resist the glossing effect of the calender stack. Finally, a calender with sandblasted rolls may be used to "emboss" the dull surface. While superficially appearing the same and having the same gloss level, these different sheets may have major differences in printing detail, ink gloss, ink drying, ink scuff, and runnability.

Letterpress

Letterpress is the oldest of the printing methods. The design to be printed is raised above the surface of the plate. Today, a large volume and variety of printed material is produced by letterpress printing such as newspapers, magazines, labels, packages, and corrugated containers. Letterpress, however, is losing its share of the printing market to the offset and gravure methods.

Paper characteristics for letterpress

Smoothness. Defined as fine pinpoint smoothness where the distances between irregularities are 1/100 to 1/200 in. apart. As a rule, this cannot be seen with the naked eye but may be readily picked up with an 8-power lens and a low-angle light beam across the surface of the paper. The presence of pits is especially harmful (Figs. 19.18, 19.19, 19.20, and 19.21).

For letterpress and for web gravure, the glossy-coated surface will be smoother and will give better detail.

As a paper surface diminishes in smoothness, the solids usually are affected first, next the halftones, and the type little or not at all. Smoothness is the most important of the paper factors affecting letterpress.

Levelness. The evenness of the surface contour where irregularities are in the order of 1/8 to 1/4 in. or even larger across and about the same distance apart. Lack of levelness usually is due to poor formation and clumping of the fiber in the basestock (of a coated sheet). It is made worse by an increase in basis weight or long fiber content. Levelness can be detected by the naked eye at a low angle and is usually most noticeable in coated cover stocks and bristols. As levelness diminishes, the halftones, especially light ones, become

Fig. 19.18 Smooth vs. rough. (courtesy of Mead Corporation)

uneven and mealy and solids may show mottle, but type is not affected to any great degree.

Cushion. The compressibility or resiliency of the paper. From a theoretical basis, cushion is important in affecting ease of makeready and printability.

Fig. 19.19 Smooth vs. rough. (courtesy of Mead Corporation)

A paper with a high degree of cushion should make up for irregularities in its own structure and plate and press motion and consequently print well and easily. In practice, no measure of resiliency under dynamic operating conditions exists. Static methods occasionally have shown some degree of correlation with printed results. However, in specific cases where a sheet had

Fig. 19.20 Smooth vs. rough. (courtesy of Mead Corporation)

been criticized as deficient in cushion and showed excessive embossing, the simplest and most effective cure is to make the paper smoother and thus automatically reduce the need for impression on the press.

Coverage. The degree to which the fibers are covered up and concealed by the coating. The fine-grained coated surface will print with more detail, more

Fig. 19.21 Smooth vs. rough. (courtesy of Mead Corporation)

holdout, greater brilliance and contrast as opposed to the fibrous uncoated surface.

Receptivity. The ability of the paper surface to absorb ink. While commonly used in reference to printability, receptivity has negligible influence on the quality of reproduction of the desired forms. However, it is of considerable importance in its effect on drying rate, offsetting tendency, scuffing and chalking of the dried ink film. It is a characteristic affecting operation and runnability rather than printability.

In summary, the factors of importance to letterpress are primarily those affecting printability rather than runnability. A good letterpress sheet must be flat, trimmed correctly, dimensionally stable, and must not pick or lint. In practice, it has been easier for the papermaker to accomplish the latter attributes (those affecting runnability) than the former ones.

The aforementioned paper characteristics apply to sheet-fed and web heat-set letterpress. Additionally, a satisfactory web sheet must not blister in the ink dryer or jam or crack on folding in the folder. For a coated sheet to run free of blisters in the dryer, one or more of the following are required:

- Low moisture content: less water present to be heated to the explosion point.
- High degree of porosity which may be obtained by:
  - Low finish: less consolidated surface
  - Low coat weight: less coating to seal the surface
  - Coating pigments which do not pack closely together
  - Coating adhesives which do not form a continuous film

Jamming in the folder may be caused by uneven tension or winding, which causes the web to wrinkle. Jamming by holes, cuts, or other imperfections causes the web to break. On occasion, excessive slipperiness (low coefficient of friction) has been found to cause jamming.

Cracking at the fold is most frequently attributed to excessive or complete loss of moisture in the dryer. Other causes of cracking at the fold are low folding strength in the basesheet, high coat weight, and high basis weight. Heavy surface sizing and high adhesive content in the coating to prevent picking are also known contributors to cracking.

Offset lithography

Originally offset lithography used a polished limestone slab with the design drawn on it with a greasy pencil. The penciled areas accepted ink; the others accepted water. Today, the design for printing is at the same level as the non-printing area of the plate. A metal or paper plate transfers the design to a rubber blanket and then to the paper. In the last thirty years, offset lithography has shown a phenomenal growth and improvement in quality.

It has deeply penetrated all printing fields and comprises over 70% of all printing in the U.S. today. It dominates medium- and short-run commercial printing and is very strong in shorter run newspaper work as well as many dailies including some long run, large city papers. Nearly all special interest magazines and the majority of books and business forms are printed by offset.

Paper characteristics for offset

Surface strength. Heavy, tacky inks are generally used since they maintain a sharper line of demarcation at the oil-water interface. Due to the thinner ink film deposited by the offset process, heavier pigment loadings are necessary to maintain color intensity, which results in higher tack inks. The rubber blanket used to transfer the ink image from plate to paper makes complete contact with the entire surface of the paper and tends to have a tacky surface (Figs. 19.22 and 19.23). Offset papers are from 25 to 125% higher in surface strength than letterpress sheets. For the same reason, the offset process has little or no tolerance for loose or lightly bound surface material on the paper. This combination of tacky ink and overall contact with the tacky rubber blanket is responsible for most of the difficulties encountered in offset printing. Blanket contamination can occur both in the printing and in the nonprinting areas which results in waste and sheet distortion.

Water resistance. The use of water on the plate and blanket (pH range 3.5 to 6.0 – average 4.5 approximately) requires some resistance to its softening effect on paper surfaces (Fig. 19.24). In an uncoated sheet, individual fibers or fiber clumps may be softened and deposited on the blanket. In coated paper, an overall "milking" or whitening effect may be present due to softening of the top coating layer or individual materials in the coating. This property becomes more important in printing on multicolor presses since the repeated dampening has a greater effect. No general agreement exists in the industry, however, to indicate how much water resistance is needed.

Nonreactivity with fountain etch. The paper should be free of materials which may leach out and change the fountain etch so that it will no longer maintain a sharp distinction between printing and nonprinting areas. Active alkalies or certain dispersing agents have been known to cause scumming or tinting.

Proper moisture content. Due to the use of water on the press, which measurably raises the relative humidity of paper after printing, it is usually necessary to manufacture offset papers at a higher and more uniform moisture level than is required for other papers. Moisture contents which place the paper in balance at relative humidities of 38 to 45% are satisfactory for uncoated papers. Higher percentages of 40 to 47% are satisfactory for coated grades. Unbalanced paper will be difficult to hold in register and may often wrinkle during printing. Considering all offset papers made in the U.S., coated and uncoated, the total spread in RH may be as wide as 30 to 50.

Stiffness. While some widely-used offset sheets do not have much stiffness, a good degree of rigidity assists more in offset regarding blanket release and

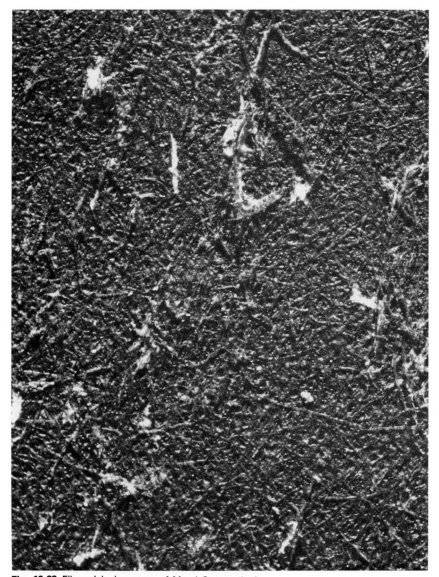

Fig. 19.22 Fiber pick. (courtesy of Mead Corporation)

better mechanical operation and production than in letterpress and gravure.

Receptivity. As in letterpress, receptivity has little or no effect on printability. To a comparable degree, however, it is of great importance in its effect on ink drying rate, chalking, and offset tendency.

Fig. 19.23 Pickout. (courtesy of Mead Corporation)

Fig. 19.24 Wet rub test. (courtesy of Mead Corporation)

As opposed to letterpress, the important offset characteristics concern runnability rather than printability. Due to the resilient structure of the offset blanket, offset printing is comparatively insensitive to differences in smoothness. Since runnability requirements are reasonably constant through the whole quality range of offset papers, differences between the top and bottom of the quality scale will be confined to superficial characteristics such as color, brightness, opacity, and other similar traits. Problems encountered in the manufacture and printing of a top-grade offset sheet will be substantially the same as those found in a low-grade sheet.

In the first few years of the move toward web offset, it was found that at least one-third or more of the web offset printers could use standard letterpress sheets with fairly good results. The balance required a sheet that was halfway between letterpress and sheet-fed offset when considering surface strength and water resistance requirements. However, as the quality of web offset work has reached very high levels and as the runs have become longer, evidence indicates that the web offset sheet should be even higher in water resistance and in resistance to whitening on the blanket than sheet-fed offset. Runs of 40,000 to 50,000 or more without a wash-up are well documented in web offset (Fig. 19.25). This is much longer than the average for sheet-fed. In regard to moisture content, the type of dryer on the web press will determine the level of moisture which may be tolerated without blistering (Fig. 19.26). Direct flame dryers are quite sensitive to paper moisture content which in some cases must be as low as 20% RH equilibrium. High velocity air dryers of modern construction are much more tolerant and will permit moisture equilibrium levels up to 40% RH. For best results, the papermaker-should be informed exactly as to the press dryer requirements.

Problems with blistering and cracking at the fold are more severe with web offset than with letterpress because the great majority of presses in use are blanket-to-blanket and print both sides at once. The printing of two wet-ink films at the same time not only seals up the surface causing the moisture to build up to higher pressures, but also applies heat to both sides at once, resulting in greater elimination of sheet moisture and subsequently, greater cracking. With the common-impression cylinder or planetary web offset press which prints and dries one side at a time, these problems are reported to be less severe.

The blanket-to-blanket press, since it applies ink to both sides of the sheet at each printing station, exerts considerable Z-direction tensile on the paper in the outgoing printing nips. This can be great enough to split the sheet and cause delamination (Fig. 19.27). At times, both delamination and blistering can occur at once and in widely-varying proportions, thus making identification and cure difficult. The cure for delamination is to increase the internal bond. This can also have a beneficial effect on blistering since it can resist the rupturing effect of the vapor pressure long enough for it to leak away. If the internal bond is increased to very high levels, perhaps by surface sizing, it can cause greater cracking at the fold since it may make the sheet hard and brittle. Some delamination in the folded area is helpful in securing good fold quality.

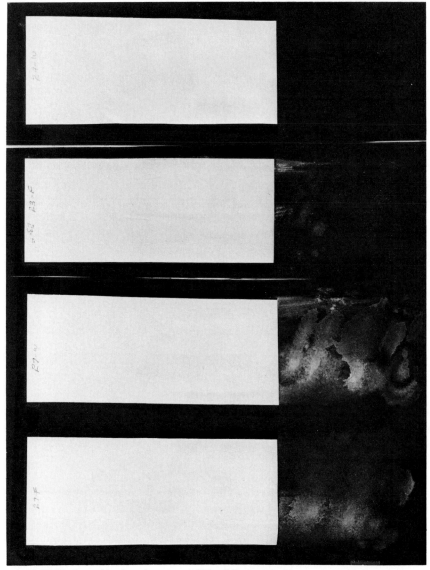

Fig. 19.25 Blanket whitening. (courtesy of Mead Corporation)

In the printing of coated groundwood sheets by web offset, a pronounced roughening of the paper surface is often noted after the sheet has gone through the press dryer. This is called *puffing* or roughening and is caused by ground-wood fiber clumps, which are small pockets of higher moisture in the sheet. These explode or at least swell due to higher vapor pressure in the dryer and

Fig. 19.26 Blistering. (courtesy of Mead Corporation)

are a form of blistering on a micro scale. Finer groundwood free of fiber bundles or gentler drying will help the problem.

Gravure (Intaglio)

Originally, the gravure process was confined entirely to illustrations while letterpress was confined to type. The design to be printed is below the level of the plate. The etchings of Rembrandt and all other engravings are examples of the intaglio process. U.S. currency and postage stamps are printed by this process as well as some deluxe advertising and a few high-grade books and reproductions of photographs. Sunday newspaper supplements, catalogs, and other mass-produced material is printed by web gravure (rotogravure). Sheet-fed gravure is the most artistic and most expensive of the printing processes while web gravure is the least expensive in long runs.

Paper characteristics for sheet-fed gravure

Smoothness. Due to the enormous pressures used in sheet-fed gravure, the

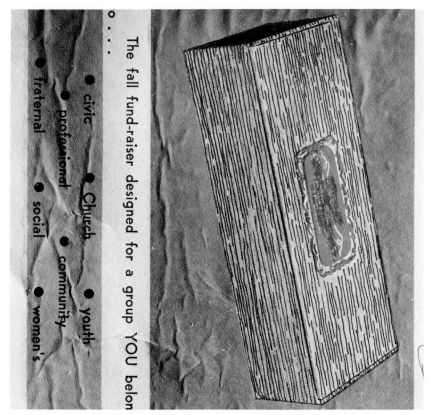

Fig. 19.27 Delamination. (courtesy of Mead Corporation)

normal measurement of fine pinpoint smoothness is only one of the criteria of quality. Good compressibility and a finely-knit surface and internal structure will produce good results even with an antique surface. Fiber morphology is also important. The finest and silkiest of commonly-used fibers is esparto, and the addition of this pulp to a gravure sheet has produced paper of top printing quality. Further, a smooth, uncoated offset sheet has shown improvement in gravure printability by eliminating surface sizing, which makes the sheet softer and more compressible.

Printing smoothness is the best way to describe the combination of fine pinpoint smoothness, softness, and compressibility and fineness of surface and structure which together give the best results with sheet-fed gravure.

Paper characteristics for web-fed gravure

Smoothness. Fine pinpoint smoothness is the most important characteristic. In the case of coated paper for web gravure, this is almost the only measure of quality. The *snowflaking* or missing dots often noted in the light tone areas of web gravure printing are due to insufficient paper smoothness. (Figs. 19.28 and 19.29) Since this lack of smoothness can be traced directly to fiber dimensions rather than to any failure in formation visual smoothness, coating spread, or gloss, it becomes much more difficult for the papermaker to correct it. Naturally, fiber dimensions have a direct effect on most of these properties, but since the dimensions themselves are a function of the wood supply, they cannot be readily changed.

Other factors which contribute to snowflaking are:
- Type of etch used. Conventional, square dot, now rarely used is better than invert halftone, round dot.
- Insufficient printing pressure.
- Soft impression rolls.
- Ink too volatile, tends to dry on the printing cylinder.

Compressibility. Only indirect evidence indicates that this is of value in web gravure. The very short dwell time in the printing nip lends support to pinpoint smoothness as the most important.

Ink wettability. A few cases where surface wettability appears to have been of importance are considered very rare and more an ink problem.

More differences between sheet-fed and web operations exist in the gravure process than the other processes. Web gravure is essentially a part of the publishing and catalog industries and is concerned almost entirely with long runs and high speed. Sheet-fed gravure, on the other hand, is a deluxe, top-quality process which has little or no connection from an economic or quality basis with its web counterpart.

The web printer is concerned with the price and high tonnage of paper. The vast bulk of this stock is either supercalendered or machine coated groundwood, with surface smoothness and mechanical condition of rolls the main interest.

Fig. 19.28 Effect of surface smoothness on gravure print quality. (courtesy of Mead Corporation)

The sheet-fed printer deals largely with uncoated papers of high quality. They range from English finishes through the medium, antique, and even fancy finishes with mellowness and good texture as the top requirements. However, coated papers, glossy, dull, and matte, also can be used.

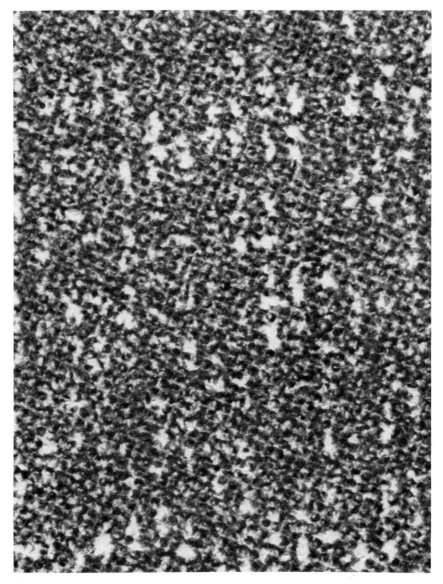

Fig. 19.29 Gravure print not contacting paper. (courtesy of Mead Corporation)

Refer to Table 19.1 for an overview and comparison of paper characteristics needed for the three principal printing methods.

Table 19.1 Paper characteristics needed for major printing processes

Paper Characteristics	Letterpress	Offset	Gravure
Smoothness level needed (for halftone print quality)	High	—	Very high
Smoothness level needed (for solids and type)	—	—	High
Surface strength needed	Moderate	Moderate to very high	Very low
Water resistance needed	—	Moderate to high	—
Stiffness needed for best operation	Moderate	High	Low
Sensitivity to paper surface (Can small changes in the chemical surface characteristics of the paper have a pronounced effect (at times) on the printing process?)	Usually never	Often very sensitive	Rarely

Screen process

In screen process printing, the design to be printed is attached to a screen which is usually silk, cotton organdy, synthetic fibers, or metal. The mesh of the screen will vary with the quality requirements of the job. Finer mesh gives finer detail.

The nonprinting areas of the screen are staged out with glue, shellac, or similar material. The ink is squeegeed through the open areas on to the surface to be printed. The actual printing operation might be a hand one (2000 impressions per day) or mechanical (2000 to 3000 impressions per hour). Web screen presses using rotary screens and up to ten colors are used mainly in textile and specialty printing, but paper for later thermal transfer to cloth is also being printed.

The screen process has a definite advantage in ease of makeready over the other printing processes and is most practical for short runs, jobs that are larger than standard size presses, or a surface or odd-shaped material that cannot be handled by any other process such as glass, metal, plastic, or heavy board.

Screen process printing excels in vividness and contrast due to the heavy ink film that can be applied. Also, enthusiasts claim that the screen process can print on anything that will ''hold still.'' It is not surprising, then, that there has not been any pronounced demand for a special screen process printing paper.

Paper characteristics for screen process

Flatness. Sheets must be free of curl, buckle, ridges, welts, and wrinkles. Any of these may cause imperfect contact with the screen and subsequent faulty reproduction.

Bulk. Higher bulk with its higher rigidity is more resistant to the warping effect of the thick ink films used.

Surface. Any type paper surface may be printed but the uncoated and rougher surfaced sheets are a little less susceptible to smearing and drying difficulties.

Dimensional stability. Paper should be resistant to shrinkage, curl, and warping, which may be encountered in the drying operation, especially in multicolor work.

Many new printing methods are in use or under development including thermal, magnetic, electrostatic, photoelectrostatic, and ink jet. Many require special paper to function at all, but even the most tolerant of these new methods will function better with papers whose characteristics have been maximized for the particular process.

An example of the high demands on paper today is the photoelectrostatic copier and/or printer. The great majority of these machines use uncoated bond-type paper in cut sizes, 8½ × 11 in. and related. The principal characteristic needed in copier paper is structural stability — primarily resistance to curl or warping under a wide range of temperature, humidity, and fusing conditions. The paper rests in the machine until use in a variety of office or shop conditions. In operation, the paper must travel through the machine (many different travel paths) and is imaged (powdered toner most widely used); the image is then fixed to the paper (using heat, pressure or a mixture of the two). New printing technologies will continue the demands on the papermakers to develop effective, low-cost, durable paper.

Section X
Testing Paper and Board for Printing

C. J. Miller, Editor

Introduction

The scientific basis for testing

Testing is a multipurpose function in which something is examined, measured, or estimated. It can be viewed as an individual science which is applied to all branches of science. As such, typical principles of science are applied in the development of many standard test methods. Some realization of how this relates to the practical business of testing is shown by the following objective steps in test development:

1. Precisely define the property to be tested.
2. Postulate a suitable test model based on performance requirements.
3. Adapt or develop instrumentation to aid senses in the test.
4. Determine the fundamental variables in the model and functional relationships between them.
5. Ascertain the property which will be the best test criterion to express an end result. Seek quantitative measurement and expression.
6. Design experiments to determine suitable levels for control of other variables, and accordingly establish a tentative standard test procedure.
7. Determine the efficiency of the test for a reasonably large sample population, including:
   a. Replication (precision) and significance of the test.
   b. Sensitivity of the test.
   c. Sampling requirements.
   d. Degree of correlation of the test with:
      (1) End performance
      (2) Other pertinent tests
   e. Unit operating time of the test.
   f. Unit cost (capital and operating).
8. Refine and reassess the test.

Test functions

The requirements of a test are dependent on the way in which it will be used. Certain tests are effective in certain functions and not in others. Typical test functions are quality audit, quality control, referee test, and research test.

Time of test is a major element distinguishing tests for quality audit from those for quality control. Appreciable rejects may be produced before they are identified in a quality audit situation. In quality control, a reject condition is identified and corrected early enough in the run to result in minimum rejected production. Correction know-how and often detailed isolation of the specific problem area must supplement the quality control test. Ideally, such tests are in-line. It is also necessary that a quality control test have a good record for prediction of end use quality.

These distinctions are important issues regarding tests for printing papers. For example, an ink wipe test may be fast enough to use in quality control, but its poor record in predicting commercial print gloss would relegate it to limited use in quality audit only. A print gloss test from proofing may be too slow for use in quality control, but its good prediction record would make it more useful for quality audit than the wipe test.

A referee test method is designed to determine which part of a system is faulty: the paper, ink, or press operation. The method must be well proven for prediction and reliability in order to achieve the referee status. An additional requirement is the availability of materials and information from the commercial run.

Research tests are used in fundamental studies and in screening laboratory developments for their commercial feasibility. Test reliability and broad coverage of properties are of prime concern in research testing.

Testing paper for printing

There are a multitude of tests for individual physical properties of paper such as basis weight, thickness, gloss, brightness, opacity, porosity, and smoothness. However, if a particular test procedure for paper quality does not emulate the printing situation closely enough it will not be a good predictor of printability. For example, a porosity test measures paper for its resistance to air flow. However, the porous property response of paper to liquid and paste inks may be somewhat different than the response to air.

Also, the effort to explain printing phenomena by direct unit relationships is an oversimplification. Print quality is comprised of several factors, each detectable as degree of defects. Each of these usually derives from different combinations of parameters. Materials are involved (paper, ink, plates, fountain solutions, blankets). Supplementary press parts may be involved (impression cylinders, ink rollers, gears, water rollers, doctor blades). Press operating variables may be involved (impression pressure, press speed, ink feed, web tension, register, ink and water balance, doctor blade angle). Various physical and surface chemical phenomena may be involved (molecular contact, wetting, cavitation, film splitting, adsorption, absorption, adhesion, cohesion). Most of these examples of items involved in the paper – ink – press interactions are general terms which support even more specific internal variables. The notion that a few isolated, relative paper tests should explain its role in this multiplicity of interaction is a bit optimistic.

Nevertheless, it is often the case that a few parameters will have major influence on a particular print quality factor. For example, the paper's effect on print smoothness (freedom from skipped print) will come mainly from its surface levelness and its surface conformability. The specific tests for those properties and their weighted influence on print smoothness are not well established. The answer is to test the print smoothness of paper by printing it under conditions that are sensitive to that property. Similar relationships have been postulated for various paper properties and other print quality factors. Many laboratories rely heavily on print testing because they have found that these tests, which simulate end use conditions, are the most reliable ones for predicting the paper quality for that use.

Classification according to printing processes

Reference to printing paper grades is often made in terms of the printing processes in which they will be used. This practice has its motivation from the specific process-oriented properties necessary to such grades. Certain printability factors such as printing smoothness, apparent ink holdout, and resistance to showthrough are general requirements for printing papers. However, the degree of the quality requirement and the mechanisms used often vary between printing processes. Process differences such as the consistency of the ink, the hardness of the printing nip, the impression pressure in both the image and nonimage areas, the ink film thickness presented and applied, and the ink drying method contribute to the degrees of quality in printing.

The ranking of papers for letterpress print smoothness, for example, is very often different from their gravure print smoothness rank. Letterpress skip occurs mainly in solid print because the paste ink has low mobility, leaving complete coverage primarily a function of the high image area pressure. Gravure skip occurs mainly in highlights because of low image area pressure and, even with liquid ink, the risk of noncontact of ink and paper increases with a decrease in cell area. Pits in the paper surface cause skip in both processes. These mechanisms suggest that pit depth may be the critical dimension in letterpress, but that pit area may be more significant in gravure. Different paper surface requirements are defined accordingly for these processes, and different methods are used to test for those requirements.

20
Tests for Gravure Printing

C. J. Miller

Introduction

Gravure printing is characterized as a "smooth" process and one in which great depth of tone is produced. The main paper requirements for gravure are ones which especially enhance those characteristics. Gravure print smoothness is defined as the freedom from missing or defective dots in tones *(1)*. The surface levelness of the paper is of prime importance for the achievement of good gravure print smoothness. Also, the conformability of the paper surface to the printing form usually provides a synergistic benefit to gravure print smoothness.

The depth of tone quality in gravure usually relates to the wide range of ink film thickness that can be printed from one form. A like range is manifested in the print appearance, quality of color, density, and gloss. Absorptivity is the paper property that most influences changes in these qualities. Showthrough and strike-through are other appearance properties affected by paper.

The gravure press is a smooth-running machine compared to those of other conventional printing processes. Thus, it is adaptable to long, high-speed runs and precise tension control. This smooth mechanical operation goes hand in hand with smooth print production. Gravure paper grades should be free of defects which interrupt that smooth operation. Reasonably good mechanical strength properties will help avoid web breaks, but avoiding processing defects such as bursts and calender cuts are equally important. Baggy webs are often considered more aggravating than web breaks to the smooth operation of the gravure press. Good tension control is disrupted by such webs, and the resulting misregister impairs print smoothness and color. The build of the roll has strong influence on the baggy web and burst problems.

Other quality factors from both commercial and laboratory prints have been researched. For example, Arnamo *(2)* evaluated print density contrast and mottling in dark tones. Blokhuis *(3)* reported results on beading. Swan

(4) dealt with mottle, wire mark, and ink refusal. Albrecht *(5)* evaluated legibility of line and type. Perila *(6)* evaluated ink requirement.

Print smoothness

Many authors *(7, 8, 9, 10)* have emphasized missing dots in highlights as the major gravure printing defect and associated it with paper surface roughness. Pritchard *(9)* termed this defect "speckle," compared its size distribution with that of paper roughness, and measured it by means of a modified Chapman smoothness tester. She determined that speckle was caused by pits equal to or greater than one gravure cell unit in area. Miller and Plante *(10)* determined that fibrous structured pits ($>60\mu$m diameter) and shives or fiber bundles (approximately 50μm $\times$ 250μm) were the paper surface anomalies most frequently associated with missing dots. Such anomalies are apparent on the paper surfaces of Fig. 20.1 (right side) in the same location as the skipped dot in the corresponding monotone print.

A reliable, objective method of directly measuring defects quickly for quality control purposes has not been developed to date. Conventional paper smoothness test instruments which measure the time for a common known volume of air to leak across a surface or instruments which actually measure air flow rate have generally been found to correlate poorly with gravure print smoothness. The Print-Surf, a relatively new air leak-type instrument developed by Parker *(11)*, tests a very small area of paper surface (about two-thirds the diameter of a typical gravure highlight dot) under impression up to 300 psi (2068 kPa) and is relatively insensitive to substrate porosity. Parker showed fairly good correlation between the print smoothness results from this instrument and gravure prints. Miller *(12)* obtained rank correlation coefficients (Spearman's Rho) of about 0.9 between the new air leak-type instrument values and the smoothness ratings from laboratory gravure prints on coated papers. On the other hand, Gunning *(13)* compared air leak instruments with the ranking of prints from the G.R.I. Printability Tester, and found generally poor correlation for all.

Gravure print testing

Laboratory gravure presses

The gravure printability of paper can be predicted most reliably from developed tests on laboratory gravure presses. Various presses have been used in the industry; for example, eleven different gravure test presses were described and evaluated *(14)*. Several bench presses have been used effectively in testing paper. Swan *(4)* described gravure proofing press and opera-

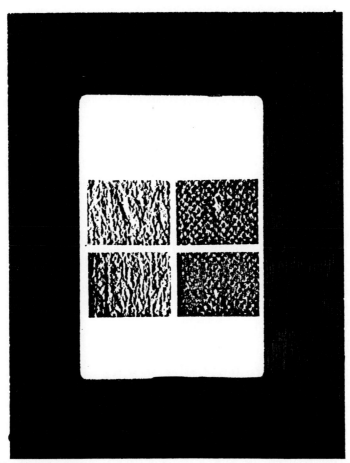

Fig. 20.1 Tests for gravure.

tion in detail. This is a web-fed press which is used widely for paper testing in Europe. Roehr *(7)* did research work and developed test methods on a gravure web press designed and built in his company's research laboratory. The G.R.I. Gravure Printability Tester was explained by Oppenheimer and Ree *(15)*. This sheet-fed press was designed by G.R.I. in conjunction with an extensive TAPPI program. It simulates typical commercial presses in many elements such as speed, nip geometry, doctoring, pressure, and ink circulation. A gravure press was modified by Miller *(12)* and compared with the G.R.I. press for practicality in testing applications.

Gravure cylinder etch

After the press is obtained, the kind of print and etch to use are of primary importance. The prints should be sensitive to the visual assessment of skip.

This should be provided for as much as possible in the etch so that unusual levels for other variables such as impression pressure are not applied. The qualities needed are:

- Large uniform highlight monotone [e.g., 2 × 3 in. (51 × 76 mm)]
- Enough distinct skip to show differences between prints
- Enough tone value to give good contrast between skip and print

Photomicrographs of prints from engraved cylinders, increasing from A to D in hard dot characteristics, are shown in Fig. 20.2. More skip results from more narrow cell width, for which cell depth must be increased to produce suitable tone value (density). These factors are well balanced for test purposes in the "D" etch. These dots appear similar to those of commercially printed gravure highlights. It must be stressed that gravure print quality may vary from one area to another, and thus tests of a small area (50 mm²)

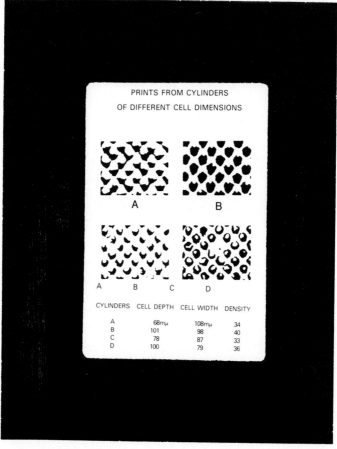

Fig. 20.2 Photomicrographs.

may be unreliable. This is frequently a problem with test objects which utilize widely-spaced lines of halftones where counts of missing dots in a given line may not be representative of the paper as a whole.

Standard test method

In order to assure print test reliability, standard methods with careful control of important variables should be developed. An ink similar to that used in the field for the paper to be tested is usually suitable. A typical ink viscosity for high-speed publication gravure is 30, Zahn cup no. 1 (7 chemically pure). A higher viscosity such as 22 sec., Zahn cup no. 2 (40 CP) is usually necessary to obtain good prints on the slower laboratory presses. The ink viscosity, impression pressure, press speed, doctor blade settings (extension, angle, pressure), ink level in the fountain, sample handling, and web tension should be specified.

The main criteria for these specifications relate to the appearance of the print. In combination, they should consistently produce the desired appearance on a standard press paper. If they do not, it is preferred to adjust the controlled variables to that end, rather than allowing shifts in the standard print appearance.

The use of reference standard prints for visual evaluations provides an objective, numerical rating system and improved repeatability to the test. For a given grade, about 4 or 5 prints cover the range of quality levels, and can be assembled in a reasonable time. About 12 reference standard prints in series become precise print smoothness rating numbers. The print to be assessed is matched to one of these standards and receives the corresponding rating. The number of missing dots increases approximately logarithmically from 0 to 300 skips/cm^2 for a 150 lines/in. tone. Bristow *(17)* has shown that perceptual threshold is proportional to the number of missing dots and that a 10% change is required to be noticeable.

Roehr *(7)* and Miller *(12)* have reported on the reliability of visual evaluations by the reference standard procedure. Nevertheless, a TAPPI survey (CA 1509) conducted in 1971 indicated a wide preference for instrumental evaluation of dot skip. This prompted George *et al. (16)* to develop a method and apparatus for that purpose. The G.R.I. rotary scanner was never commercialized, but a number of videocamera image analyzers have become available. These instruments have been shown by various authors *(18, 19)* to be of significant value, not only for gravure evaluations, but also for a wide range of print quality attributes.

Tests on solid print

Certain print defects which are related to the printability of paper are most readily detected from solid print, which should be provided for on the form.

An "off-solid" etch of about 30μm cell depth will serve well and will help in avoiding messy printing and puddling in the solid. A visual inspection of the solid print area is usually sufficient to determine acceptance or rejection of samples for defects such as mottle, ink refusal, and strike-through (reverse side of print). Poor ink drying on web presses generates blocking at the winder; this blocking is visually apparent. A useful ink-drying test can be developed on this basis by arranging conditions on the press to produce a small amount of blocking for a normally good drying material. Such a test is effective, for example, in work with water base inks, which notoriously give drying problems.

The print appearance attributes of gloss, density, and showthrough can be measured with reflection instruments. Print gloss is often measured at 75° on the standard gloss meter for paper (Specular Gloss of Paper and Paperboard at 75 Degrees, TAPPI Test Method T 480). For ink films of very high gloss, the 60° specular reflectance method for paints and plastics (American Standard Test Method D 523-53T) is preferred. It gives a lower gloss value and a greater gloss spread between such samples than is given at 75°. The "snap" demanded by advertising executives for four-color ads relates more to print gloss than to any other appearance attribute. The material and process properties relationships which produce high print gloss are very complex. Generally, the absorptivity of paper is inversely related to print gloss. Conversely, print gloss is the best relative measure of the absorptivity of paper for the ink used in printing it. Various other absorptivity tests (ink wipe, ink smear, Vanceometer oil gloss loss, oil drop nip spreading, print density, etc.) often are not reliable. Again, to determine "ink holdout" of papers, print gloss is the most reliable relative test.

Print density can be measured directly on a reflection densitometer. This measurement is highly useful as a measure of color strength. Optical color filters on these instruments should generally be used according to the manufacturer's instructions. Print density is a good relative indicator of the amount of ink transferred to the paper.

The densitometer can also be used in obtaining a numerical value for showthrough. Read the density on the reverse side of the print, after adjusting to zero with the sensing head placed on the unprinted area of the paper. The showthrough value may be multiplied by 100 so that simple whole number values can be reported. Other reflection meters can be used for obtaining a relative showthrough measurement. Alternatively, such values in terms of reflection can be converted to showthrough by converting all reflection values to density ($D = \log 1/R$).

Baggy webs and roll build

Baggy webs are generally considered to be the most important runnability problem in gravure. The roll build of paper is the paper property most closely related to this problem. RHO-meter tests in profile help in defining roll build. Similar to a hardness tester, this instrument measures hammer rebound deceleration. A typical reading on a roll of coated magazine paper is 40 points. It has been found empirically that RHO-meter profiles at 3-in. (76 mm) intervals across the roll, having a total variation of 10 points or more, tend to run to baggy webs. Such variation can sometimes be reduced by rewinding the roll. RHO-meter testing has helped considerably in correcting the baggy web problem in gravure printing.

Literature cited

1. TAPPI Gravure Section Report, February 19, 1965.
2. Arnamo, A., Sixth EUCEPA Symposium, September, 1962.
3. Blokhuis, G., *Druckspiegel* 16 (10): (1961).
4. Swan, A., *Printing Technology* (April 1969).
5. Albrecht, J. and Falter, K.A., 8th IARIGAI Conference, Aulanko, Finland, 1965.
6. Perila, O., 8th IARIGAI Conference, Aulanko, Finland, 1965.
7. Roehr, W.W., *Tappi Journal* 41 (11): 671 (1958).
8. Zentner, T.G., *Tappi Journal* 42 (3): 225 (1959).
9. Pritchard, E.J., *Printing Technology* 9 (2): (1965).
10. Miller, C.J. and Plante, P.W., *Tappi Journal* 51 (4): 180 (1968).
11. Parker, J.R., *Tappi Journal* 54 (6): 943 (1971).
12. Miller, C.J., GATF Conference on Paper Performance, October 10, 1972.
13. Gunning, J.R., *Tappi Journal* 55 (12): 1678 (1972).
14. TAPPI G.A.C., Gravure Section Meeting, September 12, 1963.
15. Oppenheimer, R.H., and Ree, J.F., *G.R.I. Newsletter* No. 21, (July 1969).
16. George, H.F., et al, U.S. Patent 3,909,138 (September 30, 1975).
17. Bristow, J.A., IARIGAI l5 Intl., Lillehammer, Norway, June 1979.
18. Heintze, H.U., and Gordon, R.W., *Tappi Journal* 62 (11): 97 (1979).
19. Lyne, M.B. and Jordan, B.D., *Tappi Journal* 62 (12): 95 (1979).

21
Tests for Letterpress Printing

W. C. Walker and J. Marton

Introduction

The characteristics of paper that determine its suitability for letterpress print-ing fall into two groups: runnability and printability. The runnability of a paper is the degree to which it can be printed on a press without operating difficulties. Runnability includes all properties that contribute to smooth passage of the paper through the press. Good runnability means freedom from strength defects, excessive curl in sheets, bagginess in rolls, dirt or "dog ears," bad splices, or any other defect that reduces press speed or avail-ability *(1)*.

The printability of a paper is the degree to which its properties enhance the quality of the prints made on it by a given printing process. Attempts have been made to treat printability as a single property and express it as a single number, but this is an excessive simplification that has had only limited usefulness in restricted situations. To effectively deal with printability, consider the paper properties of greatest significance to printability for the printing process under consideration. For letterpress printability, the two paper properties of greatest importance are printing smoothness and ink receptivity.

Printing smoothness

The printing smoothness of a paper is the ease with which it attains full con-tact with the ink on the plate with minimum pressure and ink film thickness. It is paper smoothness under the impression pressure of the printing nip. Insufficient printing smoothness results in breaks or speckles in the printed pattern, thus interfering with good print quality. Many different smoothness measurements have been applied to letterpress papers; some indicate the visual smoothness of the unprinted paper, but most have been intended for predict-ing its printing performance.

Research reports on correlations of smoothness tests on papers with their printing performance have had varying claims for success. Much of the divergence of reports is due to the different types of paper samples used. Good correlations can be obtained from almost any test using a homogeneous series of papers such as those which differ only in amount of calendering. If a heterogeneous series is used, however, with papers from different suppliers made in different ways from different materials, then good correlations with printing performance are difficult to attain.

One of the earliest tests for smoothness was gloss measurement, since it seemed obvious that a glossy surface should be smooth. This concept has been one of the reasons for the demand for high gloss from the printing industry, but correlations with printing smoothness have been poor.

In the search for more direct measures of surface smoothness, the air-leak smoothness testers were developed by Julius Bekk *(2,3)* and others *(4, 5)*. A Bekk Smoothness Tester consists of a metal cylinder with an open bottom that is set on the paper sheet with a smooth backing surface. Air is introduced into the cylinder at a standard pressure and leaks out between the bottom edge of the cylinder and the paper surface. With a rough paper, the openings are large, and only a short time is required for the escape of the standard air volume. Thus, Bekk smoothness is expressed in seconds with high values for the smoother papers. The Bekk Tester gave a better correlation with printing than did gloss, but it is subject to error for two reasons. Some air escapes through the body of the sheet as well as along the surface, and it is very sensitive to whether the surface depressions are isolated to depressions or elongated valleys that provide direct channels for escape of air. The modern version of this instrument designed by Sheffield overcomes these problems to some extent, and is also direct-reading with flow meters. While air-leak smoothness can be helpful in checking the uniformity of a specific grade of paper, its correlation with printing smoothness can be poor for a heterogeneous series of papers, and it can give erroneous evaluation of paper innovations. A recent version of air-leak smoothness testers claims a better correlation with actual print performance. The measurement is carried out under pressures approximating printing nip pressure.

Another approach to roughness has been the use of a tracing stylus that follows the contours of the paper surface with a needle and magnifies them electrically to give an accurate and sensitive surface profile. Such instruments have been developed primarily for metal finishing industries, but some *(6, 7)* have been adapted to paper surfaces. The results can be shown as a magnified profile or a mathematical function such as the standard deviation from the mean surface level. These stylus profiling techniques have been helpful in analyzing special problems, but correlating them with printing performance has been difficult. The paper is examined under very different compression conditions than those during the printing impression and the decision what numerical characteristics of the profile should be used was difficult. One of the most meaningful ways of interpreting such profile data was devised by Roehr *(6)*. He measured the fraction of the area of the paper surface that was in depressions deeper than a set limit. These are the areas most difficult to contact with ink in printing. Roehr's correlations with gravure printing were reported to be very good, but the method was slow and therefore impractical.

One approach to measuring paper smoothness under print-like conditions is the optical prism method of Chapman *(8)*. In the Chapman Optical Printing Smoothness Tester, the paper is compressed under a glass prism at pressures up to 700 psi (4826 kPa). The prism is internally illuminated at such an angle that light escapes through the lower prism face where there is optical contact with the paper surface, and is internally reflected where there is no contact. Thus, the smoothness can be determined and expressed as the percent of the paper surface in optical contact with the prism at a given pressure. This method is direct reading and shows increase in smoothness with pressure and paper improvements such as supercalendering. It is also possible to view patterns of contacting areas directly and see surface formation, wire marks, coating pattern, etc. This measurement is normally derived from the highest point of the surface that makes contact most easily with the prism or with an inked plate. In letterpress printing, however, difficulties with printing smoothness are associated with the five percent or less of the surface that is most difficult to contact.

Another approach to the measurement of printing smoothness determines the volume of ink or other liquid required to fill the roughness contours or valleys of the paper surface. This approach can give clear pictures or topographic maps of the paper surface as described by Hull and Rogers *(9)*. Such patterns were analyzed qualitatively by Lyne and Copeland *(10)* using magnetic inks; the technique has been improved by Verseput and Mosher *(11)*.

Many other methods have also been studied for the development of a bench test for the letterpress printing smoothness of paper. Success has been limited, however, by differences between what is actually measured and the performance property interest. It may be possible to get better results using a combination or battery of tests as was done by Glassman for gravure printing *(12)*. The other approach is measuring printing smoothness directly. Very high correlations with press performance have been obtained with tests that involve actual test printing and evaluation of the print defects related to inadequate printing smoothness.

Printing tests for smoothness

Printing tests for smoothness involve two steps: making prints under reproducible conditions that bring out smoothness defects and evaluating the resulting prints. Such prints can be made on small commercial presses, proof presses, or laboratory print testers. For the printing to be reproducible, it is necessary to control carefully the ink temperature and the humidity of the printing room and the pressure, ink film thickness, and speed of printing. Techniques for these controls have been described in the literature *(13)* and in the instructions with laboratory print testers. A good printer will select the printing conditions that obscure the defect in the paper surface, but for print testing one must select conditions that bring them out clearly. Thus, for printing smoothness, it is advisable to use a black ink at low ink film thickness and low printing pressure so that there are some breaks in the prints for even the best papers to be tested.

Visual examination of letterpress prints, especially solid prints made at low pressure and ink film thickness, reveals scattered small white specks caused by low spots in the paper surface that were not contacted by the ink film during impression. In commercial printing, this is the defect resulting from inadequate printing smoothness that will bring complaints from the printer. Thus, the paper giving the smallest number of specks in the print or the least "break" in the print should be rated as having the highest printing smoothness. A numerical scale for this purpose can be set up in several ways. The simplest method is to select a stepped series of standard prints representing in steps the amount of break that can be readily distinguished visually. These standard prints should be on paper similar to that which will be tested so that the appearance of the break will be similar for precise comparison. The standards are assigned numbers on the smoothness scale and a test print is given the number of the standard it matches most closely. Once a series of standards has been selected, an experienced tester can evaluate test samples on this semi-quantitative test scale very rapidly. With care, the results can be very reproducible and correlation with commercial printing performance is very high.

Instruments have been used to measure the quality of these prints, including a reflectance meter to measure the blackness of solid prints *(16)*. Breaks in the print should reduce the blackness, and thus the blacker print should indicate the paper of better printing smoothness. For closely related papers, this blackness correlates well with visual evaluation, which is the primary standard, but the correlation is very poor for comparison of unrelated papers. Another factor, the ink holdout of the paper surface, influences the blackness of the print areas which are covered with ink. Thus, the average blackness of the print, as measured with a reflectance meter, is influenced by the ink holdout as well as the breaks in the print.

Among the instrumental methods used to overcome this problem was that described by Walker and Carmack *(1)*. These authors conclude that in evaluating these prints, the eye notes those areas which are significantly different from the average blackness of the print. Therefore, they devised a scanning instrument that established the average blackness and then measured the percent of the area with blackness of more than a selected difference from the average. This percent of the area, as a measure of the amount of break, was reported to give excellent correlation with visual evaluations. For most testing, however, the direct visual evaluation is considered the most rapid and reliable.

Ink receptivity

The second most important printability property of paper for letterpress is its ink receptivity, or the converse, its *ink holdout*. When an ink film is applied to a paper surface, it does not stay completely on the surface but penetrates to a degree dependent upon ink and paper properties and other circumstances. In this penetration, the pigment particles in the ink generally stay on the paper surface, except on an extremely open sheet like newsprint. The liquid portion of the ink, its *vehicle*, can penetrate deeply, depending on the paper porosity, the fluidity of the ink vehicle, and the time available. Vehicle penetration causes an increase in viscosity of the ink remaining on the surface, and then formation of a nonfluid *filter cake* of pigment on the surface. As the vehicle drains from this pigment layer, the surface changes from glossy to dull; in extreme cases, drainage can be so complete that the pigment layer is chalky and inadequately bound. Printing inks are formulated with high viscosity, resinous components to minimize these dulling and chalky effects.

The ink receptivity of a paper surface influences letterpress printing in several ways:

- Penetration of ink vehicles during impression increases the percent of ink transferred from the plate and reduces squash-out of halftone dots.
- Penetration during impression, plus the following few seconds, improves wet trapping and the setting of inks to minimize setoff in the stack or roll at the end of the press. Penetration during this period also reduces the gloss of heat-set inks.
- Penetration over a period of minutes or hours can reduce the gloss of inks and varnishes that dry more slowly by oxidation and polymerization.

Thus, the exact ink receptivity characteristics desired in the paper depend on which of the performance results are of greatest importance for the case in hand. Generally, a compromise is sought where there is enough holdout for good ink gloss in the final print but still enough absorbency for good ink trapping and setting. It should be noted that the very short time processes are primarily influenced by paper structure very near the surface, whereas the slower processes can involve much deeper penetration.

Different methods have been devised for measuring the absorbency or porosity of paper. The simplest is probably the measurement of air permeability with instruments such as a densimeter (17). In this measurement, the paper requiring the greatest time for a standard volume of air to pass through is the densest, least porous sheet. This method is rapid and convenient and can be helpful for papers of relatively open structure that are similar throughout the sheet, such as newsprint. Air permeability is often used as a control to indicate changes in other papers such as coated papers, but it is not reliable in predicting printing performance.

A first step toward simulation of practical conditions was the use of liquid penetration tests. Some liquid tests, such as the Castor Oil Penetration Test (18) and the Patra Test (19), involve time for liquid to penetrate completely through the sheet. Again, such tests involve structure much deeper than that influencing most printing performances, and tests more specific to the paper surface have been sought. One interesting approach to this problem was an instrument, which was able to give a complete graph of the amount of an oil penetrating paper as a function of time (20). This graph gave a good picture of rates at different depths in the sheet, and its initial slope gave an indication of the penetrability of the paper surface.

The most widely used measure of paper surface permeability is the K and N Ink Test (21). A special test ink is applied to the paper surface, wiped off after a standard period of time, and the darkening of the paper surface is noted with a reflectance meter. The ink is formulated differently from normal printing inks in that the color is a dye soluble in the vehicle, instead of suspended pigment particles. Thus, the dye penetrates the paper with the vehicle, and the amount of color remaining after the surface has been wiped clean is dependent upon the amount of penetration. This test gives a good indication of the relative surface absorbency of closely related papers, but can be misleading in comparing papers made in different ways. The same amount of K and N ink penetrated into papers with different pore distribution and different pigment opacities will give different optical effects. Because of such problems, other ink receptivity tests have been devised that simulate the actual printing performance.

Ink holdout for good gloss and sharp, clean color of prints is a primary concern of the printer for many types of jobs on coated papers. Bench tests can give general guides, but many papermakers have found simulated printing tests more reliable. Such tests are normally devised by the individual laboratory based on the proofpress or other test printing unit available. A solid print is made of sufficient size for good visual inspection as well as use of glossmeters for numerical evaluation. It is important to use an ink very similar to those to be used commercially and at a similar ink film thickness on the paper. Inks formulated for other purposes, such as tack-graded inks for pick testing, can rank a group of papers in quite different order. Conditions of drying of the print are also critical and should be kept constant and similar to those in the customer's printing shop. With care, this method can give a very reliable evaluation of the ink holdout of paper.

An essentially opposite ink receptivity property of paper is its setting rate for "quickset" inks. In much sheet-fed printing, where gloss is not important, inks are used that will "set" very quickly by vehicle penetration so that the sheets can be stacked in the delivery pile without setoff or smudging. This property can be evaluated by making prints with this type of ink and watching the gloss of the solid print as a function of time. The freshly printed area will be glossy, but as the vehicle drains into the sheet, the print will become dull. This change can be quite abrupt, and the time to this point can be a good measure of surface absorbency. An instrument for testing box-board based on this principle is the vanceometer. Here, a film of standard oil spread on the board surface and glossmeter is placed on it almost immediately. The gloss is then read as a function of time and a characteristic curve is obtained. Variously defined endpoints on the curves have been used to obtain a single number for the penetration characteristic of the paper or board sample.

Particularly with the growing use of high-speed multicolor presses, the ink absorption that takes place in the first seconds or fraction of a second has become of increasing interest and importance. Extrapolation of the above methods to very short times is difficult and of doubtful significance. Several approaches have been devised to obtain data during or very shortly after the printing impression *(15)*.

The first approach is the *setoff* or blotting of printed ink films at measured short times after impression. Crude arrangements can be devised with proof-press printing, but modern print testers are more effective. These devices are arranged so that the freshly-printed paper passes through a second nip where the fresh print is pressed against a clean sheet of paper. The amount of ink transferred from the fresh print to this second sheet of paper is judged visually or by optical or gravimetric measurements. The less ink blotted off in this fashion, the more completely the ink film has set. This setoff of the ink film can be determined as a function of time, and data can be obtained for times as little as one second or less.

Ink transfer during printing

The measurement of the percent ink transfer during letterpress printing has provided insights into the mechanism of the printing process and information on the influences of the printing smoothness and ink receptivity of the paper. It shows these influences during the impression and actual print formation itself. The most precise and accurate measurements of ink transfer during printing have been made by direct weighing of the inked plate before and after impression. This data gives the ink film thickness on the plate going into the printing nip and the amount remaining on the plate afterward. It is normally expressed as *percent transfer* or the percent of the offered ink which is transferred to the paper. The techniques have been described in the literature cited *(13,22)*.

Measurements can be made readily on the print testers by weighing the plates or printing disks *(23)*. The percent transfer obtained in this way is not a constant but is normally plotted as a function of ink film thickness originally on the plate to give a characteristic curve. As in Fig. 21.1, the percent transfer rises sharply with increasing ink film thickness at first, passes through a maximum, and then falls to approach a constant level at very high ink film thicknesses. These curves are interpreted in terms of three effects taking place during impression and transfer. An equation was developed *(24)* to fit these curves that contains three constants related to each of these effects.

$$y = (1 - e^{-kx})[b(1 - e^{-x/b})(1 - f) + fx]$$

$$\text{where } x = \text{ ink on plate}$$
$$y = \text{ ink on paper}$$
$$k, b, f \text{ see below}$$

The first effect is the degree of contact of the ink film with the paper surface. At very low ink film thickness, ink only contacts the highest areas of the paper surface. At low percentage contact, low percentage transfer occurs even if the ink is transferred to contact areas. As the ink film thickness is increased up to levels normally used in commercial printing, sufficient ink reaches into the valleys of the paper surface, and the percent of contact in-

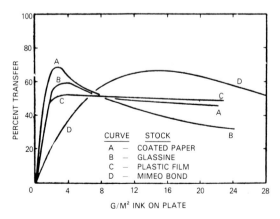

Fig. 21.1 Typical ink transfer curves for various paper stocks.

creases rapidly until the paper is completely covered by ink and the white specks in the print disappear. This increase in contact accounts for the initial steep rise in the percent transfer curve up to the maximum. The constant of the equation, k, can be related to ink transfer data in this film thickness region. It characterizes how rapidly contact increases with increasing amounts of ink and, thus, is a direct measure of the printing smoothness of the paper obtained under actual printing conditions.

The second effect is the tendency of the paper surface to "immobilize" the ink in direct contact with it during impression. This immobilization is caused by physical entrapment of ink in the rough structure of the paper surface and by absorption of vehicle into the paper pores. This loss of vehicle from the ink film increases the viscosity of the ink next to the paper surface. When the ink film is split by separation of paper from the plate after impression, this immobilized ink is more resistant to splitting than the rest of the ink film. Hence, the film split takes place in the unaffected or least affected "free ink" furthest from the paper surface. The immobilization of the ink is expressed by the constant b in the equation, and is a direct measure of the absorbency of the paper surface for the ink vehicle in the few milliseconds of an actual printing impression. At low ink film thicknesses, this effect can reach through the entire ink film and result in very high transfers where there is contact. As the ink film increases, the immobilized ink is a smaller fraction of the whole film, and the percent of transfer decreases.

The third effect is evident at very high ink film thicknesses. Here, the immobilized ink becomes a very small fraction of the total ink film, and the percent transfer approaches asymptotically the percent transfer of the free ink. The third constant in the equation, f is the fraction of the free ink that goes to the paper. This fraction is very seldom 50%, as would be expected for random rupture or split in the middle of the free ink. On a proof press, it has been found to be 40-45% for coated papers and as low as 20% for certain carton boards *(25)*.

Measurements of ink transfer have revealed many properties of paper that influence letterpress printing. Unfortunately, the techniques require too much time and care to provide useful control methods, but this approach does provide a useful research tool, and several subsequent studies have been made *(26, 27, 28)*.

Uniformity of paper surfaces

Most properties of paper are generally measured and discussed in terms of a single average figure for the whole surface. In many cases, however, the distribution of this property is as important to the printer as its average level.

A good example is gloss. All commonly available glossmeters give an average gloss for the paper surface, but when the gloss of paper is examined visually, the eye sees gloss patterns or gloss mottle. Printers and other paper users are frequently more strongly influenced by the intensity, size, and distribution of glossy spots on the paper than they are by the average levels that are measured. Considerable technology in the measurement and characterization of variations in the opacity of paper has gone into the development of formation testers, and one day will be regularly applied to other surface properties. A recent symposium included discussion of various solutions for instrumental evaluation of solid and halftone prints. *(31)*.

Variation of ink holdout over paper surfaces is an important printing property that is difficult to measure in meaningful terms. This variation can result in very objectionable variations in the gloss of printed solid areas or in the tone density of uniform halftones. One way to show ink receptivity variations in paper surfaces is to observe the patterns in the smears used for the K and N ink test. One can readily see patterns that are quite different from one paper to the next, but are not revealed by numbers from the reflectance meter. The interpretation of these patterns, however, is still a matter of opinion.

Surface strength

One property where variation over the paper surface is of particular importance is the surface strength of the paper. In the printing process, the splitting of the ink film during the rapid separation of paper from the plate exerts substantial stress on the paper surface that depends on the tack of the ink and the rate of separation. If the paper is not strong enough for this stress, it will rupture in one of several ways. Mild failure can involve pulling out poorly bound pigment from the coating or pieces of coating. Blisters can form from partial failure of bodystock, poorly bonded fibers or fiber bundles can be pulled out, or the entire sheet can be split or torn. Since even a small amount of such failure can ruin a good printing job, printing papers must be free from *picking*. In other words, while the average surface strength must be high enough, it is the weak end of the strength distribution curve that is of primary concern.

One of the oldest and most widely used methods for measuring the surface strength of paper is the wax pick test *(29)*. In this test, a series of numbered sticks of wax graded in cohesive strength are used. Several sticks are selected; their ends are melted, pressed against the paper surface, and allowed to cool. When the sticks have cooled, they are pulled sharply away from the paper to test its strength. If the wax is stronger than the paper, pieces of the paper will be pulled away by the wax. The strongest wax that a paper can withstand is taken as a measure of its surface strength.

While the wax test is a useful guide, it has shortcomings that have led to the development of a number of pick testing instruments. The hot wax can disrupt thermoplastic components of paper such as latex binder in coatings. The area tested is very small so that the average strength level is found rather than the weakest, which may be widely scattered. Also, the application of stress is different from actual printing, where the area is all stressed at the same time. In the hot wax test, the peeling action of the paper comes from a roll nip where only a thin line on the paper surface is stressed at any instant. In a fibrous material like paper, a stressed element on the surface can gain support from unstressed elements near it, but if all are stressed at the same time, this support is not as available. This hypothesis is supported by the fact that many papers have poorer pick resistance in the cross-machine direction than in the machine direction, presumably because of their fiber orientation.

As with other properties, inadequacies of bench tests have led to the development of printing tests for picking. Proofpress tests were developed with controlled ink properties, ink film thickness, pressure, and speed, but they proved to be cumbersome, and smaller printing devices were built to make the work faster and simpler. One of the major problems in print testing for picking is to find and define an endpoint. For a given ink tack and press speed, the test paper will either fail or not fail, and conditions where failure starts must be found and defined. Testing with a series of inks similar to the waxes is difficult, since the press must be cleaned and reinked for each ink change. Therefore, finding the limiting speed for a given ink was more practical, but still required many tests on the same sample to find the endpoint.

The development of the accelerating pick testers helped to find and define an endpoint. With these instruments *(30)*, a single print shows the picking effects of a wide range of printing speeds. As the speed increases along the print, a point is reached where the paper starts to fail. The speed at that point and the viscosity or tack of the ink is used to define the pick resistance or surface strength of the paper. Picking tests such as this can be very useful for letterpress printing if they are performed with care. The method is not as useful for lithographic papers because testing is done without water and a very small area of the paper is examined in determining the endpoint so that widely scattered picks, especially serious in lithography, are not detected.

Another important factor to remember in all print testing of paper, especially for picking, is that inks can interact seriously with roller distribution systems. Soft rollers can either absorb liquid components from inks to increase their tack, or exude into the ink plasticizers or wash-up solvents to reduce the tack. This effect is of very little significance on commercial presses where there is a continuous flow of fresh ink through the roller distribution system to flush out altered ink. In a small test distribution system where a single initial charge of ink is run to equilibrium with the rollers, it is the altered ink that is used for the testing and not necessarily ink supplied in the can or tube. One way of avoiding this difficulty is to use drawdown techniques to apply ink at proper film thickness directly to the printing plates. Such equipment is available for both flat plates for proofpresses and printing disks.

Conclusion

A great deal of work has been done and reported in the literature cited on measuring some of the paper properties most important to letterpress printing. There is a whole field of letterpress printing with rubber or other soft plates known as flexography, where many considerations are quite different. The soft plates conform under pressure to contours in the paper or board surface so that the printing smoothness of the stock is not nearly as important. Also, the inks are frequently based on alcohol or other highly volatile solvents so their behavior and handling requirements are quite different. With development of small test "flexo" presses, it is true that any printing process must be closely simulated to get meaningful printability test results.

Literature cited

1. Walker,W.C., and Carmack, R.F., "The Printing Smoothness of Paper," *TAGA Proceedings* **15**: 235-58 (1963).
2. Bekk, J., "Apparatus for Measuring Smoothness of Paper Surfaces," *Paper Trade Journal* **94** (26): 41 (1932).
3. Technical Association of the Pulp and Paper Industry, "Smoothness of Paper (Bekk Method)," T 479, TAPPI PRESS, Atlanta.
4. Bendtsen, C., "New Testing Methods and Instruments for Determining the Quality of Printing Paper," *Pulp and Paper Magazine of Canada* **41** (1): 20 – 26, 43 (1940); (3): 232 – 234 (1940).
5. Simmons, R.H., "Paper Testing and Printing," *Paper Trade Journal* **120** (24): 35 – 38 (1945).
6. Roehr, Walter W., "Effect of Smoothness and Compressibility on the Printing Quality of Coated Paper," *Tappi Journal* **38** (11): 660 – 664 (1955).
7. Hull, H.H., "An Adaptation of the Proficorder for Paper Printability Studies," *TAGA Proceedings* **14**: 118 – 37 (1964).
8. Chapman, S.M., "The Chapman Printing Smoothness Tester. I. Basic Development and Recent Modifications," *Pulp and Paper Magazine of Canada* **55** (4): 88 – 93, 104 (1954); *Tappi Journal* **38** (2): 90 – 96 (1955).

9. Hull, H.H., and Rogers, M.C., "New Methods for Observing Properties of Paper which Influence Printability," *Tappi Journal* **38** (8): 468 – 472 (1955).

10. Lyne, L.M., and Copeland, D.E., "Print Quality Evaluation by Magnetic Scanning," *Tappi Journal* **51** (8): 363 - 372 (1968).

11. Verseput, H.W. and Mosher, R.J., "A Simplified Printing Smoothness Test Using Magnetic Ink," *Tappi Journal* **54** (8): 1309 - 1314 (1971).

12. Glassman, A., "Predicting Paper Printing Quality by the Battery of Tests Method," *Tappi Journal* **44** (1): 7 - 11 (1961).

13. Fetsko, J.M., Walker, W.C., and Zettlemoyer, A.C., "Techniques for Controlling Laboratory Printing Conditions," *American Ink Maker* **33** (10): 34 (1955).

14. Technical Association of the Pulp and Paper Industry, "Proof Press Test Procedure for Printing Smoothness," TAPPI Useful Test Method UM 466, TAPPI PRESS, Atlanta; "Use of the I.G.T. Tester to Predict Printing Smoothness," TAPPI Useful Test Method UM 505, TAPPI PRESS, Atlanta.

15. Swan, A., "Realistic Paper Tests for Various Printing Processes," *Printing Technology* 9 –22 (1969).

16. Larocque, G., Axelrod, B.l, and Clark, S., "Measuring the Printing Quality of Newsprint," *Pulp and Paper Magazine of Canada* **52** (3): 166 - 174 (1951).

17. Technical Association of the Pulp and Paper Industry, "Air Resistance of Paper," TAPPI Test Method T 460, TAPPI PRESS, Atlanta.

18. Technical Association of the Pulp and Paper Industry, "Castor Oil Penetration Test for Paper," TAPPI Test Method T 462, Atlanta, TAPPI PRESS.

19. Wass, W.H., "The Powdering Problem in Lithography," *British Printer* **63** (377): 36 - 39 (1951).

20. Anon., "Measuring Instruments," *American Pressman* **66** (3): 34 - 36 (1956).

21. Casey, James P., *Pulp and Paper Chemistry and Chemical Technology*, second edition, Vol. III, Interscience, New York, 1961, p. 1718.

22. Fetsko, J.M., and Walker, W.C., "Measurements of Ink Transfer in the Printing of Coated Papers," *American Ink Maker* **33** (7): 38 (1955); *TAGA Proceedings.* 130 - 138 (1955).

23. Fetsko, J.M., "Comparison of Ink Transfer Measurements on Four Laboratory Print Makers," *Advances in Printing Science and Technology* Vol. II, Pergamon Press, New York, 1962, p. 164 - 168.

24. Walker, W.C., and Fetsko, J.M., "A Concept of Ink Transfer in Printing," *American Ink Maker* **33** (12): 38 - 40, 42, 44, 69, 71 (1955); *TAGA Proceedings* 139 - 149 (1955).

25. Taylor, J.H., and Zettlemoyer, A.C., "Hypothesis on the Mechanism of Ink Splitting During Printing," *Tappi Journal* **41** (12): 749 – 757 (1958).

26. Schaeffer, W.D., Fisch, A.B., and Zettlemoyer, A.C., "Transfer and Penetration Aspects of Ink Receptivity," *Tappi Journal* **46** (6): 359 - 375 (1963).

27. Hsu, B., *Advances in Printing Science and Technology* Vol. II, Pergamon Press, New York, 1962, p. 89.

28. Karttunen, S., *Paper and Timber* 1970 (4a) 159.

29. Technical Association of the Pulp and Paper Industry, "Surface Strength of Paper (Wax Pick Test)," TAPPI Test Method T 459, TAPPI PRESS, Atlanta.

30. Technical Association of the Pulp and Paper Industry, "Surface Strength of Paper (IGT Tester)," TAPPI Test Method T 499, TAPPI PRESS, Atlanta.

22
Tests for Offset Printing

N. R. Eldred

Introduction

Two features of offset lithography require special properties of paper. First, the nonimage area of the plate is kept clean with water, and because water may be transferred to the paper, offset papers require a certain amount of water resistance. Second, the offset blanket contacts the entire surface of the paper running through the press, requiring that offset paper be clean, strong, and stiff. Being flexible, the blanket conforms to roughness and irregularity in the sheet, and sheet smoothness is less important in offset lithography than in letterpress or gravure printing.

As with all printing papers, optical properties, moisture content, and bulk properties are important to offset papers, and together with all web papers, heat resistance — resistance to blistering, fiber puffing, and cracking at the fold — is important to web offset papers.

It is more difficult to distinguish the differences between printability and runnability problems with offset papers than with gravure or letterpress papers. Lack of smoothness causes a printabiltiy problem with gravure and letterpress while poor roll conditions cause web breaks and shut down the press, a runnability problem. Typical runnability problems of offset papers such as spots, hickies, and picking, require the pressman to shut down the press and clean up, thus blurring the distinction between offset printability and runnability.

An offset press is an important device in the evaluation procedure for determining the suitability of paper for offset printing, and a press is used by most papermill quality control departments. Evanoff *(1)* reports that some offset presses have good capabilities for measuring picking, piling, and blanket contamination, and fair capabilities for measuring mottle, streaks, and uniformity, but they are of little value for measuring water resistance, ink gloss, plate wear, and ink drying phenomena. However, test development must be based on field experience. Test procedures or groups of test procedures must separate paper samples into acceptable and nonacceptable groups in agreement with field experience. In other words, "To measure paper performance, we must print it," still applies in testing of offset papers.

Communication standards

Lack of adequate communications inhibits social and economic progress, and the printer and papermaker have suffered from the lack of communication. Different printers, often in the same city, use different terms to describe the same problem, much to the confusion of the papermaker who tries to determine whether or not his paper may have contributed to the problem. For example, piling may describe the accumulation of paper fibers or pigment particles from either paper coating or filler in either the image area or the nonimage area of the offset blanket. Dusting, linting, and milking also describe certain aspects of this phenomenon. Linting has also been used to describe the loosening of fibers on the surface of the paper. *Communications Study: Suggestions for Better Communications Between Designer/Art Director and Graphic Art Supplier* (Atlanta: TAPPI PRESS, 1969) and *Glossary of Paper Terms for Web and Sheet-Fed Offset Printing* (Atlanta: TAPPI PRESS, 1971) were published to help overcome the confusion. Glossaries are also available from the British Standards Institution and CPPA, and more frequent use of these reports and glossaries would improve communications and greatly aid in the understanding necessary for the reduction of printing problems.

Runnability

Problems such as scrap in the skid, dog ears, short sheets in sheet papers, and poor or unmarked splices and uneven rolls in web papers are clearly runnability problems causing down time, smashed blankets, and customer complaints, but they have nothing to do with the way the paper takes an image. There is no test for these problems that substitutes for the watchfulness of the operators in the papermill. Production personnel must be responsible for preventing or eliminating the problems and keeping defective paper from reaching the customer. A good training program is as essential in producing paper that performs properly as is a good testing program.

Cleanliness

Although freedom from dirt and debris is important for all printing papers, cleanliness of offset papers is especially important because the offset blanket contacts every square centimeter of paper running through the press and frequently picks up dirt and prints it on image after image. Fig. 22.1 shows an extreme example of slitter dust caused by improperly operating slitters.

Bits of coating, paper, or dirt, which fall onto the sheet before it is calendered, become embedded in the surface and usually remain there until the paper is printed. Fig. 22.2 shows bits of paper on an offset blanket on press. The defect resembles picking, except that a dry blanket exerts sufficient force to remove the calendered mill dirt.

Other sources of contamination attributable to paper include dusting, linting, and piling *(2)*. Dust can often be detected on sheet paper by lifting a sheet or two off the skid and wiping over the next sheet with a piece of black velvet *(3)*. Low angle illumination, may also reveal dust or lint on the surface of the paper. The GATF dry dusting test *(4)*, which measures the change in the color of a dry, black blanket after running 100 sheets on press, gives

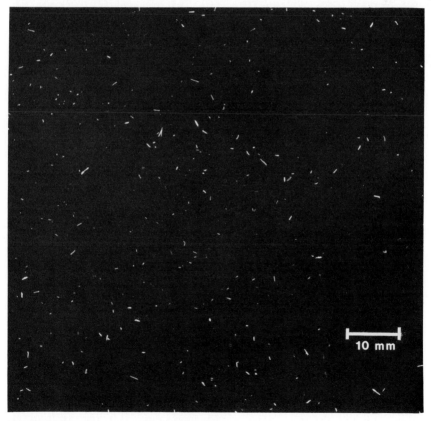

Fig. 22.1 Slitter dust on an offset blanket (2X).

Fig. 22.2 Micrograph of a pickout.

a numerical estimate of dust, lint, and loose particles. As with skid and roll defects, it is best to deal with contamination problems by preventing their occurrence with a well-trained, alert crew. Nevertheless, it is necessary to test for unbonded or loosely bonded dirt, paper fibers, and pigment particles. An offset press is the best device.

The building of paper particles, usually mixed with ink, on the offset blanket is referred to as *blanket piling, coating piling, milking*, or simply *piling*. With uncoated papers it is called *linting (2)*. It is one of the most troublesome problems associated with offset papers. Because the phenomenon involves paper, ink, blanket, and other press parameters, it is not uncommon for a given lot of paper to cause problems on one or two presses and not on others. Furthermore, the problem often comes and goes from day to day, on a given press, using a given lot of paper. It is, therefore, impossible to predict the occurrence of blanket piling, but the relative tendency of two papers to cause dusting or blanket piling can be tested. Laboratory methods have been reviewed by Eldred *(4)* and by Kantrowitz and Ray *(5)*. Measurement of surface strength and moisture resistance may also be useful, but testing for blanket contamination is best performed on an offset press *(1, 6)*.

At this point the papermaker is in a predicament. No laboratory test matches all of the variables of the offset press, and the press itself is a variable. No two presses operate in exactly the same manner. Like every complex piece of machinery such as an automobile or a paper machine, each press has its own individual characteristics. Fortunately, however, it has been found that by maintaining the press under the strictest possible control, it is possible to gain meaningful information about the behavior and characteristics of paper. Evanoff *(1)* discusses the effect on press behavior of changes in blankets, blanket wash, fountain solution, press speed, printing pressure, ink coverage, and related variables.

Surface strength

Determination of surface strength, or "pick" resistance, is of prime importance in testing of offset papers because offset lithography demands greater strength of paper than do other methods of printing. A number of tests for dry strength are presented in TAPPI Test Methods as shown in Table 22.1.

Surface strength is related to the bursting or tensile strength, but the significance of these properties in predicting the performance of printing papers has not been determined. T 403 and T 404 are often used in the evaluation of printing papers. There is a tendency to run tests simply because "we've always done it that way," or to use testing equipment because it is on hand. The quality control department must continually review the testing program and eliminate tests that give poor correlation with pressroom experience.

Water resistance

Because of the variability in the ways that offset presses are operated, it is especially difficult to predict to what extent moisture will affect paper on

Table 22.1 TAPPI test methods for dry strength

Test Method Number	Title
T 459	Surface strength of Paper (Wax Pick Test)
T 514	Surface Strength of Coated Paperboard
T 499	Surface Strength of Paper (IGT Tester)
T 403	Bursting Strength of Paper
T 404	Tensile Breaking Strength and Elongation of Paper and Paperboard (Using Pendulum - Type Tester)